T0348306

Survive the Modern World

How VEGANISM CAN SAVE *Us*

Emma Hakansson

Hardie Grant

BOOKS

INTRODUCTION

If you've picked up this book, chances are you recognise that while there is so much good in the world, we're at risk of losing it all if we don't take action. As the latest report from the United Nations' Intergovernmental Panel on Climate Change (IPCC) makes so abundantly clear, the climate crisis is unequivocally caused by human activity. In the same vein, we can't wait to be saved: this is going to have to come from ourselves. We're going to need to act fast, too – the climate crisis won't wait for anyone.

While there's no single solution to such a complex problem as a world riddled by environmental destruction, tied up with issues of racial injustice, gender-based violence and normalised brutal animal cruelty, veganism can certainly help to save us.

The oldest definition of veganism was documented around 1944 by The Vegan Society, which today defines veganism as:

'... a philosophy and way of living which seeks to exclude – as far as is possible and practicable – all forms of exploitation of, and cruelty to, animals for food, clothing or any other purpose; and by extension, promotes the development and use of animal-free alternatives for the benefit of humans, animals and the environment. In dietary terms it denotes the practice of dispensing with all products derived wholly or partly from animals.'

Today, the benefits of veganism for the environment are particularly important because we all share the one planet, full of rich, stunning, finite natural 'resources' which we need to live and thrive. Without a steady climate, biodiversity or fresh water, there will be no animals – human or otherwise – to exploit, or to come to care for.

Many people ask if veganism is so great, if it really is such a strong and viable solution to some of today's most important problems, why aren't we talking about it more? And how do we make this change, for the sake of the planet and all life on it? Well, let's explore that.

The ice caps are melting at an alarming rate. Flash floods, wildfires and other natural disasters are becoming frighteningly commonplace. Colourful, gem-like corals are bleaching into white skeletons. Native insect, fish, bird and mammal species are declining faster than ever before. Sometimes, living on this planet can feel pretty scary and hopeless.

There are direct causes of these mammoth problems and, with them, solutions. It seems as though with every passing year, or even month, the recognition that animal agriculture is inherently unsustainable becomes more wide-reaching and inescapable.

Many voices echo this same message. The global Animal Rebellion activist movement, a branch of Extinction Rebellion, is combating the climate and ecological crisis with a specific focus on the impacts of animal agriculture, and government refusal to address them. Vice-President of the United States Kamala Harris has expressed her interest in educating the US population on the environmental impact of how we eat, with meat being an important aspect of this. Organisations like Greenpeace are calling for agricultural transition away from animals, and for plant-based food systems. The UN has called animal meat 'the world's most urgent problem', with the IPCC declaring a plant-based transition to be a 'major opportunity for mitigating and adapting to climate change'.

It's clear our relationship with animals, and what it means for our relationship to the planet, is something that is being taken very seriously. If we're to take it seriously ourselves though, and if we're to bring any of this into our own way of living, we need all of the facts. So why is it that animal agriculture is so detrimental to the wellbeing of our planet?

Part One

SAVING THE PLANET

7

Chapter One

The Climate CRISIS

The rundown on biodiversity

Not to be dramatic, but everything is ruined if we don't have a biodiverse planet. Without a wide and unique range of different plant and animal species, ecosystems will collapse. Right now, we're in a biodiversity crisis. We're seriously lacking. Today, according to the UN, about one million species are threatened with extinction.

We are living in what many scientists refer to as the Anthropocene Epoch, the period of time in which one species, Homo sapiens, has evolved into a threat to the lives of the majority of all others. There have been periods of mass extinction before; in fact, this is the sixth one that we know of. We all know about when dinosaurs became extinct, and even though that extinction period wasn't the largest – that was the one at the end of the Permian era – it's hard to fathom that what our society is doing to the planet, and to all those animals and plants living on it, could be categorically similar to the wiping out of the dinosaurs. And yet this is exactly what we are doing.

According to the study 'Accelerated modern human–induced species losses: Entering the sixth mass extinction', species are becoming extinct at a rate significantly faster than that which has been recorded for the past millions of years before. Sixty per cent of primate species are threatened with extinction because of one primate species – us. We are just 0.01% of life here, yet since the 1970s, we've wiped out 60 per cent of all animal populations, according to a major report by WWF. Another study, led by Professor Ron Milo, found that we've caused the loss of 83 per cent of all mammals. If we look at the IUCN Red List of Threatened Species, we can see that we've already killed off a Great Barrier Reef island residing rodent named Bramble Cay melomys, the Pinta Giant tortoise, the Mexican Dace ray-finned fish, the Christmas Island pipistrelle bat, the Splendid poison frog, the Saudi gazelle, and the Kaua'i'ōʻō honeyeater bird, to name a few.

This 'biological annihilation' is not due to ancient climatic patterns, to chance, or to anything other than our actions. The amount of greenhouse gases we have released into the atmosphere, the number of trees we have cut down and land we have cleared all play a part. A significant and not to be overlooked cause of this is our exploitation of animals, largely for food and fashion.

Biodiversity loss and the animal industrial complex

The animal industrial complex – the system that breeds, grows and 'transforms' animals into food, furniture and fashion – has a lot to do with biodiversity loss. Professor Milo's report found that of all mammals left in the world today, 60 per cent are those referred to as 'livestock' – farmed, commodified animals like cattle, pigs and sheep. After farmed animals and humans, only four per cent of mammals left on Earth are those who are wild and free. Tigers, elephants, koalas, chimps, wombats, bears – they're all in that four per cent.

Farmed chickens, who largely spend their lives in rows of cages or stuffed into crowded sheds, make up 70 per cent of all birds in the world. For every cockatoo, crow, crimson rosella, crowned eagle or other free bird you see, there's an absurd amount of chickens you don't – except, perhaps, when they're sitting on your plate.

A big part of the problem here is that the billions of animals we farm and kill need somewhere to stand and food to eat while they're living. Half of all habitable land – so forget glaciers and barren land – is used for agriculture, and of this land, 77 per cent is used for grazing animals for slaughter, factory farms and crops grown to feed these animals.

This system leaves little space left for nature. Yale's Global Forest Atlas states that the ranching of cattle for beef and leather, for example, is responsible for 80 per cent of the deforestation and destruction of the Amazon Rainforest – the lungs of the Earth. This deforestation increases further if you include the soy production linked to it, which predominantly goes to feeding factory-farmed animals, including farmed fish and pigs, and cattle in feedlots around the world. Soy milk in your coffee won't seriously hurt the world – inefficient animal agriculture does.

Greenhouse gas emissions

They're the most talked about piece of the climate crisis puzzle, and farmed animals belch and pass them. Greenhouse gases, which are warming the planet, are significant in the animal industrial complex.

Before we get to the belching, though, let's talk more about land clearing, degradation and deforestation. World Resources Institute data tells us that in 2019 we lost a football pitch of untouched, pristine forest every six seconds. Government data shows that 54 per cent of Australian land use is for animal grazing alone. Sixty-three per cent of European arable land is used for animal agriculture and 85 per cent of the UK's agricultural land is tied to the rearing of animals. In the US, 41 per cent of land use in the contiguous states is related to animal agriculture. That's an awful lot of the world being eaten up.

This doesn't just seriously impact biodiversity, but our climate through carbon emissions, too. Trees are priceless. They provide us all with breathable air, they provide homes to many animals and they help entire ecosystems flourish, while sequestering – pulling in and securely storing – carbon from the atmosphere. They are over one-third carbon and have the ability to turn carbon into oxygen through photosynthesis. When we cut them down, the carbon stored inside them is released into the atmosphere, causing temperatures to rise further. If we want to stick to the Paris Agreement, which aims to combat the climate crisis by ensuring our emissions reduce, we need to stop cutting down so many trees. To prevent a global temperature rise, we need to both dramatically reduce our emissions going forward, and remove greenhouse gases from the atmosphere today. Sequestration helps with removal and it's for this reason we must protect our forests.

But what can we do to reduce our emissions? This can be a daunting question, considering that, based on Oxfam reporting, the richest one per cent of the world are responsible for over double the carbon pollution of the poorest 50 per cent, and just a handful of companies are massively responsible for such a large amount of global emissions. It can make us feel helpless when governments around the world continue to prioritise short-term economic growth rather than building a more secure, sustainable society.

But we do have power. The Food and Agriculture Organization (FAO) of the UN produced a report called 'Livestock's Long Shadow' stating that the greenhouse gas emissions relating to the animal agricultural sector are more significant than the emissions which come from all transport fuel exhaust. Think of every car in peak hour traffic, every ship, every truck, every plane in the sky burning fossil fuels. This is a hugely significant and confronting statistic because it means there are serious changes we – billions of us – can make, in the way we eat and dress, to do our part within an enormous movement for sustainability and regeneration. It also means we know what industries need to be held to account.

 # EXPLAINER

What's unnatural about sheep grazing meadows?

There's an argument that free-range farming, or the consumption of animals who are not factory-farmed, is more eco-friendly. Nitrogen and phosphorus released through the manure of factory-farmed animals like chickens, pigs and even fish can end up in waterways and cause eutrophication. This can lead to dead zones where near no marine life can survive.

Terrible as this is, free-range farming is not the solution, and often means more land eaten up for grazing. Animal farming always requires more land than plant-based farming, but why should we care about land being cleared if grass still gets to grow there? The reality is that rolling green pastures are unnatural. In fact, such landscapes are in a state of arrested development, says Dr Helen Harwatt. They are unchanging, not sprouting new shoots of life, or offering animals refuge. Nitrogen fertiliser is often put onto this land to keep it the way it is, and the hooves of non-native farmed animals erode the soil. It's because of these impacts that the widespread roaming of farmed sheep for wool and meat in Patagonia Park nearly saw its desertification, and the grasslands of Mongolia are at risk of vanishing due to the rising cashmere production.

Even if it is a bit depleted by grazing, the green grass still may appear natural – it might look lush. But what is really there? Largely one grass species, perhaps some trees, one species of farmed animal bred for slaughter. This is not natural, there is none of that precious biodiversity we need here. There is not a wide range of plant species to attract different insects and it's unlikely there are many small native rodents and mammals, or different birds who enjoy eating an array of bugs. Without this biodiversity, plant diseases are a greater risk, less nutrients in the soil and, ultimately, less of what really is 'natural'.

What we think of as 'natural' is often not really so. Dr Harwatt believes the reason for this, and for our obliviousness to ongoing destruction of global ecology for the sake of animal farming, is due to 'shifting baselines' between generations. 'Our parents and our grandparents will probably remember different insects and animals compared to what we remember, or they might remember more of an abundance of them ... but we have grown up in a much more barren and depleted ecosystem, so it's seen as normal.' We can't allow 'normal' to continue to mean more barren, more depleted.

The UN warns that without change now, we will reach a tipping point, leading to turbulent and catastrophic irreversible planetary changes. The worst-case scenario for our climate in 2050 is one where the air is thick, clogging our skin, making breathing difficult. In this scenario, many regions would be unlivable and many people would live through summers that reach 60 degrees Celsius. It's a not-so-far-off future where extreme hurricanes, caused by increased air moisture and sea temperatures, decimate vulnerable communities. Some of which will be forced to flee, to seek refuge, their homes under the ever-rising sea.

We cannot allow shifting baselines to fool us into thinking any of this is natural, unpreventable.

Enteric fermentation

We need to act on methane. Why? Because, as reported by the Environmental Defense Fund, this greenhouse gas is eighty-four times more potent than carbon in the short-term, warming our atmosphere for about twelve years, rather than carbon's one-hundred-year, if not much longer, impact. While emissions that hang around for as long as carbon are deeply troubling, we need to seriously reduce the amount of greenhouse gas in our atmosphere immediately. We must look at our short-term as well as our long-term strategies.

What's this got to do with animals? A large amount of methane is tied to farming animals for food and fibres because of a process called enteric fermentation. This is a more scientific term for cows, goats, sheep and other animals passing gas and belching. These ruminant animals, who have multiple stomachs – four, to be exact – have no idea how powerful and harmful their unconscious, everyday gas-passing really is. Government data shows 73 per cent of Australia's reported methane emissions are due to farmed animals passing gas. Almost 20 per cent of the United States' reported human-caused methane emissions are due to cattle. In the United Kingdom, methane emissions have reportedly decreased since 1990, largely due to fewer farmed animals being bred.

The Department of Primary Industries, an agriculturally focused government department of one Australian state, has reiterated that 'methane has a higher global warming potential than carbon dioxide, but it also has a much shorter half-life, so reducing methane now will have a much faster impact on global warming potential in the future.' Addressing farmers, they added, 'if you want to reduce enteric methane emissions, you can increase the proportion of land area under cropping'.

The climatic need for less animal farming, and so for less financial support of it through the purchasing of meat, dairy, eggs, leather and wool, is clear.

If by 2050 we have transitioned to a global, plant-based agricultural system:

- Fossil fuel emissions from about the **LAST 16 YEARS** could be removed from the atmosphere

- Greenhouse gases equivalent to 99–163% of our carbon emission budget to 1.5 degrees Celsius could be sequestered

Matthew Hayek, Helen Harwatt, William Ripple and Nathaniel Mueller: 'The carbon opportunity cost of animal-sourced food production on land', Nature Sustainability

Why regenerative agriculture isn't as great as it seems

Regenerative agriculture is great, but supposedly regenerative animal agriculture? Not so much.

Regenerative agriculture itself is super important. Essentially, it's agriculture that is not only sustainable but healing to the natural environment and to soil health. It works with natural ecosystems. It's not actually new, just repackaged. It's the kind of agriculture many indigenous peoples across the world practiced for so many years before their countries were colonised, and often still practice today.

Today, some examples of more regenerative agricultural practices include the use of rotational and diverse cropping, which benefits soil bacteria and reduces disease threats; the use of cover plants between nut and fruit trees protecting soil from erosion; and the reduction and removal of chemical pesticides and fertilisers, with farmers instead fostering an ecosystem where bugs naturally keep in balance with each other.

This is all great, but here's where it gets less great: the argument that we don't need to transition away from animal farming, we just need to do it 'better'. There's lots of talk of regenerative animal farming, of rotational grazing. It's said that by rotating grazing cattle and sheep through pastures, land is able to rest, to sequester carbon, and even make animal agriculture carbon negative. It's claimed that animals are an essential part of any ecosystem, so it makes sense that agriculture must involve animals, should it be truly regenerative. Their poo is magical, their hooves are very helpful, agriculture is nothing, let alone regenerative, without the breeding of farmed animals.

It's very easy to nip this one in the bud. While some animal agriculture is less impactful than others, the widely applauded 'regenerative', rotational grazing of farmed animals has been found not to cause a meaningful net reduction in greenhouse gas emissions as has been claimed. The 300 sources noted in the landmark report 'Grazed and Confused?' show that there is a reduction in emissions compared to conventional animal-based farming operations, but emissions would be far less if they were simply plant-based instead.

Animals are critical to the health of an ecosystem, but the animals we need are native species who should be protected by law and left in peace.

The inefficiency of animal agriculture

What would be a lot more productive in our efforts towards a sustainable, regenerative future than green-washed animal agriculture, is acknowledging the inefficiency of these systems, and what we could be doing if we evolved beyond them. So let's look into it.

We live on a finite planet, but too often act as though there is a never-ending supply of everything, as though we can continue taking from the Earth without consequence. This is not true. Earth Overshoot Day marks the date when 'humanity's demand for ecological resources and services in a given year exceeds what Earth can regenerate in that year'. In 2021, despite some reduction in our impact on the planet due to the ongoing effects of the pandemic, Earth Overshoot Day fell on July 29th.

We must do better. So how can we live well while using less? What we eat and what we dress in is a good place to start. Half of all habitable land is used for agriculture, and 77 per cent of that land is being degraded for the sake of animal consumption. Despite this, the largest report on the impact of food on the planet, 'Reducing Food's Environmental Impacts Through Producers and Consumers', published in the journal *Science* found that animal-based foods offer only 18 per cent of the world's calories and

37 per cent of total protein. When we use grain to feed animals, grown on land which could instead cultivate a whole range of crops for human consumption, National Geographic found that per 100 calories, we get only twelve calories back from chicken carcasses, ten calories back from pig carcasses and three calories back from cattle carcasses.

The same *Science* report found that the transition to agriculture that feeds us fruits, vegetables, fungi, grains, nuts and pulses instead, and which grows plant fibres rather than those off the backs of beings, would free up 75 per cent of our agricultural land while still nourishing and providing for us all.

We MUST change our diet. The planet can't support BILLIONS of meat eaters

Sir David Attenborough

 # EXPLAINER

Rewilding

Rewilding is a natural solution to a human concocted problem which simply means allowing nature to regenerate itself. At first perhaps with our help, through the planting of native trees and plants, but then, by largely leaving it to do its thing.

Imagine if all the bare grass pastures for grazing, cramped feedlots and concreted factory farms were replaced with thriving grasslands, bush, and forests full of an abundance of different indigenous grasses, plants, trees, flowers, fungi, mosses, insects, mammals, reptiles and fish. Imagine if this land became refuge and home to native animals too, often displaced and struggling due to habitat destruction. This can be achieved through rewilding.

This biodiversity also benefits our currently warming climate because the use of land for inefficient animal agriculture incurs a 'carbon opportunity cost' of sorts. A study published in *Nature Sustainability* projects that if by 2050 we had transitioned to an entirely plant-based agricultural system, we would see the sequestration, or long-term, secure and sustained storage of greenhouse gases, equivalent to 99–163 per cent of our carbon emissions budget. This budget is the total amount of carbon emissions we have left before it's all out of our hands. In other words, with this action alone, we could see a 66 per cent chance of limiting global heating to 1.5 degrees Celsius.

This would all be possible through ecosystem restoration, which would lead to carbon sequestration. This, combined with the also necessary clean energy revolution, would be utterly future-changing.

Fortunately, the money for this sort of rewilding driven biodiversity regeneration, as well as for the transition from animal to plant farming efforts, already exists. Except that right now, Food and Land Use Coalition reporting tells us money is instead being used to heavily subsidise and prop up animal agriculture, and is paying for the negative effects of this toxic system on our health. With enough community pressure on leaders, and individual action taken every day to support a plant-based agricultural system, such as through our choices in food and clothing which forgo the animal-derived options, this is a future we can have.

EXPLAINER

The impact of fishing

Every day, more fish are caught and killed than there are humans living in China, Nigeria, North America and Europe combined – a near 2.7 billion individuals, according to the organisation Fish Count's calculations. Take a moment to grasp the enormity of that.

We treat fish as worthless, replenishable goods, and their ocean home as both a mine and a dumping ground. The Census of Marine Life concluded that 90 per cent of large fish species are already gone, with more facing extinction, and it's almost totally due to human action and inaction. UN data states that 90 per cent of sea areas where fish previously lived are now devoid of fish, or heading that way.

A *Nature Communications* study titled 'Over 90 Endangered Fish and Invertebrates are Caught in Industrial Fisheries' is shocking even before we get to the body of the work. Over six per cent of all marine fish species are categorised as threatened with extinction by the International Union for the Conservation of Nature's (IUCN) Red List of Threatened Species. An Oceana report states that endangered fish are often mislabelled at sale, meaning it's impossible to know if you are eating an animal to extinction.

Southern bluefin tuna are majestic creatures who soar through the sea, growing as large as 2.5 metres and ageing up to forty years.

Yet as a species, these fish are critically endangered as listed by the IUCN, and continue to be torn away from their ocean homes. Rather than preserve the species for the sake of these individuals and their ecosystem, an independent fisheries consultant featured in the documentary *The End of the Line* shared that they are being frozen in warehouses, presumably so that they may be sold for a (literal) killing when the species inevitably is hunted to extinction. National Public Radio documented one bluefin tuna carcass sold for USD$3 million in 2019. It is immoral that animal extinction should be profitable.

From an environmental perspective, biodiversity is just as important under the sea as it is on land. Without fish, the entire ocean ecosystem would fall apart. If we make fish extinct, the species that rely on their existence for food, like some whales and sharks as well as dolphins, seals and penguins, would die out too. Without all these species supporting the symbiosis that is nature, algae, kelp, plankton, krill and worms would seriously struggle too. A barren ocean would mean barren land too. The ocean is the reason this planet is habitable, with our seas producing up to 80 per cent of the world's oxygen. If we want to continue to inhabit the planet, the oceans need to be protected.

What fishing really looks like

Picture someone fishing. Chances are, you've imagined something that looks nothing like the way fish today are generally captured. There are a few main ways industrial fishing takes place: bottom trawling, purse seine net fishing, long-line fishing and gill nets.

Bottom trawling

Perhaps the best-known of the fishing methods due to its environmental destruction, bottom trawling sees a net dragged across the ocean floor, entrapping species. These nets aim to capture squid, prawns, flathead fish and other sea animals. As these weighted nets are dragged, all species minding their own business in their deep-sea coral homes, and the corals themselves, are entangled, destroyed and killed. Bottom trawling is kind of like bulldozing an entire part of an underwater forest.

Purse seine net fishing

Another common method of fishing sees a large boat locate a school of fish and, using a crane, capture the entire school in a net that pulls closed like a drawstring bag. Government fisheries organisations state that these enormous purse seine nets can be up to 2,000 metres long and 200 metres deep (6,561 by 656 feet). The FAO describes these nets as able to capture up to 1,500 tonnes of tuna fish, which, by weight, could equate to over 43,400 individual skipjack tuna fish, or over 8,500 full size yellowfin tuna in one fell swoop. These nets are also commonly used in the salmon industry.

Long-line fishing

Depending on the depths at which they are placed, long lines are used to catch all kinds of animals, like tuna, cod and swordfish.

True to its name, long-line fishing sees lines that extend across tens of kilometres cast into the ocean. Up to hundreds of thousands of sharp hooks are strung along these lines that reach up to one-hundred kilometres long. These lines are left out for hours before they are reeled into ships with animals trapped upon them.

Gill nets

Sometimes referred to as 'walls of death', these nets are a few kilometres long and are invisible to fish. When fish, sharks and other sea animals swim into these nets, they pull back, desperate to escape. As they pull, fish and sharks get caught by their gills, fins and spines. This is often painful, injury-inducing and, unsurprisingly, stressful. Nets like these are used to capture saw and gummy sharks, rebranded more palatably as 'flake', often bought at fish and chip shops, as well as many other kinds of fish globally.

'By-catch' species

A net can't discriminate between different animal species. A whopping 40 per cent of the total worldwide capture of sea life is 'by-catch', unintentionally caught species who get caught up in careless commercial fishing operations. Oceana found that some operations throw more dying and dead 'by-catch' species back into the ocean than they bring fish back to land. While it's thought that approximations are wildly underestimated due to a lack of documentation from the fishing industry, it is estimated that each year 300,000 small whales and dolphins, 250,000 endangered and critically endangered turtles and 300,000 seabirds die each year as by-catch.

Endangered fish species, as well as long-living, slow-breeding species like turtles, small whales, seals and dolphins, suffer greatly this way. Seals and seabirds like endangered albatross die too, as well as starfish, crabs and other animals who live on the seafloor. Horrific images online of drowned birds with long-line hooks in their mouths, net-entangled turtles and dead sharks on ships show just how serious this problem is.

Many fishing operations use controversial FADs (fish aggregating devices – kind of like fish magnets), which entice fish towards their ships and boats. These greatly increase the number of species that are killed at any given time. Whenever a hook or net is put into the ocean with the intention of capture, there's no certainty of who will be stuck inside the net or on the end of the line.

If you want to address climate change, the FIRST thing you do is protect the ocean. And the solution to that is very simple: LEAVE IT ALONE

Sea Shepherd's captain Paul Watson

EXPLAINER

Farmed fish

Knowing the ecological horrors and enormous number of deaths caused by open-sea fishing, some people turn to farmed fish. However, the choice to support farmed fishing, or aquaculture, is an unsustainable one. Aquaculture is factory farming for fish. Farmed fish are bred and raised indoors, and then either live indoors for their entire lives in tanks, or are pumped into sea pens.

Sea pens, also known as cages (though that doesn't sound as good in an advertisement) aren't very big compared to the natural habitat of fish. Salmon normally swim hundreds or even thousands of kilometres in their lifetime. One Australian welfare-approved fish farm confines salmon in cages 240 metres (~787ft) in circumference and at least 5 metres (~16ft) deep. These are considered the biggest in the world. Fish here are packed in tightly, with three large, soon-to-be-slaughtered salmon fish confined to each cubic metre (~3ft^3).

We'll get to the ethical implications of aquaculture later, but right now, let's talk inefficiency, infestation and pollution. Did you know that, as found by the 'Fishing for Catastrophe' report, one-fifth of all fish caught from the wild are fed to farmed animals, including fish? One kilogram (2.2lbs) of small fish who are made into fishmeal powder must be fed to 'produce' 1.2 kilograms (2.6lbs) of salmon flesh. So if the destruction of the ocean worries you, aquaculture isn't a good alternative.

Just like factory farms on land, sea cages filled with fish result in a lot of waste – fish faeces – which can cause eutrophication, damaging the balance of surrounding ecosystems. In a similarly destructive manner, fish farms can cause infestations in wild fish populations. Sea lice, which eat away at the flesh of fish who end up covered in lesions due to overcrowding, infest overpopulated cages, and can even be passed onto wild populations who live nearby, according to reports from the *Journal of Fish Biology*. It's partly because of this parasitic transmission that the BBC reports Scottish wild salmon populations to be at their lowest levels ever, despite no commercial fishing of the species in the UK. In Canada, regions saw 95 per cent of wild, juvenile salmon populations killed by lice infestations. In Argentina, salmon farming has now been banned to protect the environment and those living in it.

It's time we leave fish alone. But don't worry – there's plenty else to eat.

Chapter Two

Healing
The
PLANET

The future of food

The future of food is green. Some people argue that to eat sustainably, we must eat locally. It's true, eating local foods is a great thing to do as it reduces food-miles – how far your food has travelled to get to you, and the emissions associated with that – and doing so supports local economy and community. However, an article from *Our World In Data* shows that people who see climate change as a major threat to their country (around eight in every ten people around the world) should focus less on where their food comes from, and more on what it actually is. It's time to dispel the myth that eating the eggs from just out of the city, or the 'free-range' meat from the family-owned farm is more ecologically responsible than eating plant-based foods – yes, even if they are shipped from the other side of the planet.

If we want to get into the specific numbers, the CO_2 emissions from most plant-based products are ten to fifty times lower than most animal-based products. Transport distance, specific farming methods used in production (back on the regenerative agriculture train) and even packaging (hello plastic, you're bad but somehow not the worst here), are often far less significant than the food type itself. Eggs, farmed fish, dairy, farmed prawns and all forms of animal meat are more impactful than any plant-based foods like soy milk, peas, nuts and corn.

The future of food is plant-based, and also lab-grown.

The future won't be sustainable unless it is JUST, FAIR, HEALTHY and NONVIOLENT. We all have a part to play in bringing this world about

 # ACTION

Stock your kitchen with vegan staples

There are a few foods that are great to keep in your kitchen and pantry that can build the basis of climate-friendly, plant-based meals. There are of course vegan meats and cheeses, but for the sake of simplicity and price accessibility (though these foods are becoming more widely available and even matching the price of their animal counterparts), let's stick to straight plant stuff.

Big disclaimer that I am not a chef, and don't actually enjoy cooking. I do like eating though! I'm also alive and healthy, and with these foods you can make a lot of different things. Have a walk through wherever you get your groceries and see what else you stumble upon.

IN THE PANTRY PROTEINS

* Lentils (great for curries and bolognese)
* Black beans (delicious in burritos and tacos)
* Cannellini and kidney beans (perfect for minestrone)
* Both silken and firm tofu (for stir-fries, scrambles and every need – tofu can become anything with the right methods and flavours)
* Chickpeas (blend with nori sheets to make 'tuna' or use in curries)

✳ GRAINS AND CARBS

- ✳ Pasta (without egg, like most dried pasta), brown and white rice, rice, udon and soba noodles
- ✳ Potatoes. Lots. (For everything from jacket potatoes to Japanese curry to potato and leek soup)
- ✳ Flour (to combine with oil and plant milk for a delicious cheesy bechamel sauce to go with lasagne or nachos)

NUTS, SEEDS, SAUCES AND SEASONINGS

- ✳ Chia seeds (great for putting into smoothies and last a long time)
- ✳ Brazil nuts (good source of selenium, only need a couple a day for that brain power)
- ✳ Sesame seeds (a yummy garnish)
- ✳ Nutritional yeast (bad name for good, B12-rich stuff to add to things for a cheesy vibe)
- ✳ Passata

IN THE FRIDGE

- ✳ Your choice of plant milk, be it soy (my personal pick), oat, or something else. The long-life milk section of the supermarket has the cheapest versions.
- ✳ Lots of vegetables. Broccoli, pumpkin, brussels sprouts – whatever you like.
- ✳ Dark, leafy things like lettuces, spinach and kale. (Good for iron, as is vitamin C, like orange juice, which helps with absorption. Wilt them and enjoy in meals, make chips out of them, blend them into a smoothie.)
- ✳ Vegan butter. (Nuttelex is my go-to. The coconut-based one doesn't taste of it while being palm oil-free.)

ACTION

Eat completely animal-free for a meal, a day, a month

We humans don't always love change, even when it's for the better. It can seem daunting, but it doesn't need to be. Let's start with a simple question. What do you eat for breakfast? If you have cereal or muesli, swap out the dairy for plant milk.

If you're more of a toast person, swap out the butter and still enjoy your peanut butter, your baked beans (most are vegan), or your jam. Make a smoothie packed with fruits, maybe some leafy greens, plant milk and maple syrup for sweetness.

Once you've tackled a plant-based breakfast, try lunch and dinner. Once you're doing it a few times a week, do it more regularly. Or just cut it out in one go, if you're that kind of person. Many meals can easily be made vegan. Google your favourite meal and 'vegan' and see what happens. Enchiladas? Yes. Shepherd's pie? Yes. Laksa? Yes. Some cuisines are already largely free from animals. Find out if your favourite is one of them.

Eating vegan food can be exciting – you can discover new ingredients, new flavours, new meals. Or you can keep it very simple. If you love bolognese, don't reinvent the wheel. Buy a plant-based mince, or make bolognese with lentils and finely chopped vegetables. Once you learn a few little cooking tricks, you won't miss the things you used to eat. Bonus points: invite a friend over to share the meal and do your part for the planet together.

Why we need to talk about animal-free fashion

When we hear about sustainability and the impacts of animal agriculture, too often we aren't hearing about the impact of what fills our wardrobes. This doesn't make sense because leather and wool, as with all animal materials and foods, have a shocking impact on the planet.

Almost everyone talks about the issue of microplastics in fashion due to the rise of synthetic materials. This is a problem, but when looking at the environmental impact associated with the production of different materials, those made of animals are far worse, according to Sustainable Apparel Coalition's Higg Material Sustainability Index. In fact, silk, alpaca wool and cow skin leather are the three most environmentally impactful materials. All other animal materials are close behind, and even the most common alternative to leather, synthetic polyurethane leather, has around seven times less impact than leather made from cow skin.

All of this matters because leather, wool and down are not by-products of the meat and dairy industries, but valuable 'co-products', if not the primary source of income, as is the case for many wool growers. The global leather goods market for example, is set to be worth nearly USD$630 billion by 2025. This idea that cow skins are used purely to reduce waste is absurd – nothing that isn't profitable would be acted out by an industry that is inherently unsustainable, cruel and capitalistic.

Collective Fashion Justice's Circumfauna project found that to produce one pair of leather boots, at least 66 kg of carbon equivalent emissions (CO_2e) are released. That's like charging 8,417 smartphones. Even polyurethane synthetic leather boots, and the impact of their supposed incineration at their 'end of life' (if they aren't able to be recycled) emits less than half those emissions: 9.5kg of CO2e. Again, that's almost seven times less.

If you're more interested in water scarcity, the same organisation reports that a cow skin leather tote bag has a water footprint of over 17,000 litres, more water than someone would drink in over twenty-three years. As I write this, I haven't drunk as much water in my life as was required to produce that leather tote bag I used to carry. Estimates suggest that synthetic leather is about fourteen times less impactful when considering water footprint and production, and pineapple leaf leather, cactus-based leather, cork and other vegan alternatives to wearing skin are also far less thirsty.

If we compare Australian cotton and Australian wool – because Australia is a significant exporter of both, and is in fact the largest exporter of wool – there's lots to look at too. Circumfauna also found that producing a wool-knit garment requires 367 times more land to be, and stay, cleared than if that same garment were made from cotton. That's a lot of lost koala and other native animal habitat. While almost all materials have their pitfalls, these are staggering comparisons.

Innovation in animal-free fashion

There are so many exciting alternatives to animal materials in fashion. Many of these materials can be sourced more ethically too, considering not only the planet, but animals and people. Instead of a wallet made from cow skin leather, which may well be made from a cow raised on cleared Amazonian land, tanned in India and shipped to be finished in Europe for the *Made in Italy* label, we have wallets made from apples, pineapple leaves and cork.

While synthetic leather is already far less ecologically impactful than animal leather, it's not the answer to the question of how to produce sustainable fashion goods. Three of the most exciting leather alternatives available today are those made from cacti, cork and mango. Desserto Pelle creates their cactus-based leather, grown from rainwater and fostering native biodiversity where it is grown. Cork, which can be dyed and made into beautiful, sturdy belts and shoes, comes from trees that don't need to be cut down for harvest, just peeled back in a bark-removing process which keeps sequestered carbon. The creation of mango leather has seen just some of the 45 per cent of globally grown and discarded fruit waste turned into stunning bags. Mushroom leather is coming out into the world now too.

When it comes to wool, there are sustainably produced forms of cotton being grown, recycled cottons, biodegradable, thermo-regulating materials like Tencel and hemp blends; there are even beanies made from recycled plastic retrieved from the garbage-filled ocean. There is silk made from discarded orange peels and rose petals, and down made from man-made, biodegradable fibres that are just as warm and more water-resistant. In the case of fashion, plants and innovation are the future. And it looks good.

*Every individual MATTERS – every individual has a ROLE to play. Every individual makes a DIFFERENCE

Jane Goodall

How to extend environmentalism beyond the personal

We all have a responsibility to reduce our harm as much as possible, and to do our part in this enormous global shift towards a just and sustainable future. However, a movement for a more just, ethical and sustainable world must exist beyond us too. We as individuals make up a collective, and only together can we make lasting, effective change. If we can't come together and support one another in making a better world, we simply won't have one.

We need to think outside of ourselves and our actions. There are many people who are less able to live vegan due to a lack of access, disability, or some other reason. Too often, these people are used as a justification for our own lack of change. Instead, we could see issues of accessibility as problems to be overcome, barriers to be removed. A sustainable food system, a sustainable world, will only ever be so if it is available to the masses.

Journalist and activist George Monbiot, on a panel featured on the BBC while talking about sustainability, explained this big problem very clearly:

'What we have to do is the big, structural, political, economic stuff. What we've been told to do is change our cotton buds, all this pathetic, micro-consumerist bollocks, that just isn't going to get us anywhere. There are one or two things you can do as a consumer that do make change. Switch to a plant-based diet, that's one, because animal farming has a massive environmental impact. Another one, stop flying. But beyond that, actually everything we have to do is change this system, we have to overthrow this system that is eating the planet with perpetual growth.'

This message went viral and while it may be shocking, there's enormous truth in it. These small changes like using a canvas tote bag rather than plastic bags, or buying non-leather shoes are important, and they do make a difference, but it's only one part of the solution. If we don't address the system that causes our root problem, which produces plastic and leather, and never-ending amounts of it, it won't be enough. If we don't address and dismantle the systems in place which uphold animal agriculture and the land degradation, deforestation and emissions caused by it, it will continue to exist and destroy. It will continue to find ways to stay relevant and profitable. We need vegan burgers to provide alternatives, but we need much, much more than that.

Agricultural subsidies

How could the destructive animal industrial complex continue to exist if we all ceased to support it? It's a good question, because claims that it would continue to exist go against the basic principle of supply and demand. However, this is exactly where the problem lies. Supply and demand is, in many cases, tampered with.

Taxpayer-funded subsidies for animal agricultural enterprises exist in America, the United Kingdom, across the European Union, in Canada, Australia and so on. These often exist due to powerful industry lobbyists who exchange funds and deals with politicians to ensure funding and pro-animal agriculture legislation. So what does all of this really mean?

Despite the fact that I fiercely oppose everything about factory farming, animal slaughter and the environmental crisis these massively contribute to, when I pay my taxes, I fund it. Despite not having bought any animal products for years, my tax money buys into them. Yours does too. In Australia, the government matches an enormous amount of animal industry funding for research, development and even marketing. For example, in 2018–19, Meat and Livestock Australia was given about AUD\$80 million from the Australian Government – from taxpayer money – just for research and development. The peak bodies for each animal 'product' – like pork, wool, and even the live export industry, receive the same kind of matched funding and support.

The system is rigged in the US too. For decades, animal farms have been protected in that if their revenue drops, the government will simply cash them out through 'revenue guarantee' programs, thus killing supply and demand's usual weeding out of industries that people no longer want as a part of their society. It doesn't matter if less people are drinking cow's milk, the farms will keep slaughtering calves and milking cows just to pour it down drains and get paid (that's cheaper than sending it to people who are hungry). Similar taxpayer-funded support of animal slaughtering industries harming our planet exists across Europe, where Greenpeace found nearly a fifth of all agricultural subsidies go to animal industries despite far more vegetable, fruit, seed and cereal crops being produced. In Canada, government data shows that only 11 per cent of all agricultural subsidies go to plant-based farming and production, with a whopping 72 per cent going solely to the dairy industry and the other 17 per cent going to the remaining animal slaughtering systems.

If we don't address this system, and the subsidies that support the current status quo of agriculture, we won't see change. These subsidies could be used to support a plant-based transition, the rewilding we so desperately need, carbon sequestration and farming schemes, or efforts to move to renewable energy. This money is ours as individuals and as a society. We need to work together to ensure it is used in a way which benefits us all, which protects us and all who live on this planet.

Grassroots movements for plant-based change

Today, individuals around the world are mobilising and banding together to address the impact of animal agriculture, and the systems which support it. One such group of people fall under the name Animal Rebellion. A mass volunteer movement that is organised, but decentralised and autonomous, Animal Rebellion uses nonviolent civil disobedience as a tool to demand that governments around the world declare a climate and ecological emergency. They further seek government action to halt biodiversity loss and greenhouse gas emissions, recognising that without a just and sustainable plant-based system, we will not be able to reach net-zero emissions by 2025 and evade ecological breakdown.

Anyone is welcome in this movement, and while it just makes sense that people be vegan to align their personal actions with those of the cause and future they stand for, Animal Rebellion recognises that for some, this is not always entirely possible in the broken system we operate within. Change of the scale that is necessary to see a just food system is massive, complex and multi-faceted. Everyone has a role to play, whether it be one of civil disobedience, of advocacy, of barrier breaking or of something else. We need people who will ensure that environmental discussions are veganised because without addressing animal agriculture, we cannot curb this crisis. We need people who will grab the attention of the media to disperse messages, people who will hold politicians accountable, people who will run for politics themselves. A community of like-minded people can change our world for the better. Historically, you only need 3.5 per cent of a population to do it.

 # ACTION

Make eco-friendly, animal-free consumption accessible

Community-focused activism is a great way to get personally involved in making the most sustainable and fair way of eating and living more widespread, and available to those with less privilege or resources. Here's how you can make veganism accessible:

* Organise with your local meal centre to make vegan food for people in need of a nourishing meal
* Organise a vegan food drive
* Offer free cooking classes or tutorials in person or online, showcasing easy, affordable and nutritious meals made with staple foods
* If you are producing vegan products, make them as affordable and accessible as possible
* Get involved in or set up a food co-op
* Get involved in urban gardening and growing initiatives
* Create freely available, factual resources about plant-based nutrition, recipes and shopping habits
* Request more affordable, plant-based food products and meals in your local grocery food stores, cafes and restaurants
* Request more plant-based foods in your local school, hospital, or other spaces
* Donate your time or money to initiatives making sustainable, plant-based food more accessible
* Call and write to your local government representatives and encourage them to make plant-based foods more available to everyone in your community

Part Two

SAVING HUMANS

Chapter Three

VEGANISM CAN HELP HUMANS DIRECTLY

Protecting the environment protects people

It is obvious that when we protect the environment, we protect people. It is clear that should we have a future as a species, we need a habitable planet. Clean air to breathe, a climate we can survive and thrive in, soil to grow food from, and clean water. It is perhaps less obvious, but extremely important to note, that the people who cause the least harm to the environment will often face the harshest consequences of our human-made climate crisis.

While people in Western and consumer-driven countries operate in a system which pushes for infinite growth, production and financial gain, people in countries who live more harmoniously with their surroundings will bear the brunt of the climatic impact of our habits. Factory farming, oil mining, an endless supply of fast fashion clothes made by exploited people out of exploited animals, and plastics which end up as fish food; these are all symptoms of a system that is greedy, and that costs planetary and human wellbeing.

Did you know that people Indigenous to the Pacific Islands are threatened by the 'extreme risk' of climate crisis, that some of their island home countries may in the next ten to fifteen years become 'submerged under water', according to the United Nations? Or that the World Bank estimates that without intervention, by 2050, across Latin America, sub-Saharan Africa and South-east Asia, 143 million climate refugees will be forced to leave everything behind for safety?

Environmental racism

Even within the borders of places like Australia, the United States and the United Kingdom, it is Black, Indigenous and other people of colour who experience the impact of our planetary harm most extremely. This is not a coincidence, but a form of racism.

Cory Booker is the first African American senator from New Jersey. He is a crusader for racial and environmental justice, and vegan. Booker focuses heavily on environmental racism, and has referred to environmental injustice as yet another 'assault on Black bodies'. One of these assaults takes place in North Carolina, where the majority of pig farms in America are placed near Black communities. Here, faeces are sprayed over fields, making the air smell 'like a decomposing body', according to residents. This isn't only deeply unpleasant to live amongst, but dangerous, with this pollution likely contributing to 'higher ... infant mortality, mortality due to anaemia, kidney disease, tuberculosis, septicaemia along with the lowest life expectancy levels in the state', according to a study in the *North Carolina Medical Journal*.

Similarly, our desire for leather means that a lot of animal skins are tanned, most often with carcinogenic chemicals like chromium, as well as arsenic and formaldehyde. These chemicals are harmful to humans, animals and the planet. Tannery workers, who in some cases are children, suffer cancer at high rates and face chronic coughing, skin ailments and other diseases. When these chemicals are released into waterways, as they often are, surrounding communities who drink and bathe in this water are harmed, as are land animals and fish.

The Earth Pledge Foundation found that US companies have moved 95 per cent of their tanneries overseas to avoid environmental oversight penalties. Today, two of the countries which tan the most leather are China and India, with the

* You become EMOTIONALLY dead

A slaughterhouse worker quoted in Yale Global Health Review on coping with such a violent, distressing job majority of their leather going to the United States and Europe, and to other consumerist countries like Australia. Communal areas in top tanning country China have been referred to as 'cancer villages' due to the effects of tanning and other industrial activities. Every day, 22,000 cubic metres – or 22,000,000 litres – of untreated wastewater flows through major tanning country India and into the Ganges River, where people drink and bathe.

None of this would be considered acceptable if these people were white.

Indigenous land rights, sovereignty and animal agriculture

Factory farming and intensive animal agriculture is a white invention, one that didn't exist before colonisation. That means that today, the intensive cattle ranching that is eating away at the Amazon is taking place on land belonging to the Waiapi Tribe, the protectors of the Amazon Rainforest. Corporations make billions from the sale of beef and leather on stolen land, and often with forced labour, according to Fashion Revolution. In *Dark Emu* by Bruce Pascoe, 17th century colonists on stolen, so-called Australian land are quoted reporting the severe impact imported sheep have had on land and edible vegetation. Today, the majority of land use in Australia is tied to the grazing of farmed animals. All of this land is stolen from First Nations people, as sovereignty was never ceded. This land has been cleared of native flora, indigenous and endangered animals have lost their homes, and First Nations people have been told they are not free to exist on the land their ancestors have coexisted with for so long before any white person or hooved animal came here.

Slaughterhouse work is largely done by vulnerable people

No one wants to work in a slaughterhouse. No one dreams of killing for a living when they grow up. If we think about this for a moment, it's perhaps not surprising that vulnerable, marginalised individuals are made to do this dirty work for the rest of us.

The British Meat Industry states that upwards of 62 per cent of slaughterhouse workers in the United Kingdom are migrants. In the US, a large portion of these workers are also migrants, refugees and oppressed Black, Indigenous and people of colour. Often undocumented, these workers are less able to stand up for themselves for fear of deportation.

In Australia, government reporting shows that migrant and refugee slaughterhouse workers from non-English speaking countries and workers with low education levels are common. 'Express entry' to the country was offered by the Canadian Meat Council to any refugees who would work in a slaughterhouse.

Some say that these people should get a different job that isn't so violent. It's easy to say that. It's harder to help ensure alternative jobs, justice and support are available for these people. Through our consumption, what we support and our own activism, we can make a difference to these people. Why is it so important alternative jobs be offered to people working in slaughterhouses? Let's walk through it.

Slaughterhouse work and the physical risks

Working in a place where death, decapitation and disembowelment are just regular parts of the job is, unsurprisingly, dangerous. Data obtained by the non-profit Bureau of Investigative Journalism found that in the United Kingdom, two slaughterhouse workers are injured every week on average. Across six years of documentation, 800 workers suffered serious injuries, seventy-eight people required amputations and four people died. Health and Safety Executive labelled the industry one of their top concerns. In Australia, there are two amputations required every single week, while in the United States, one quarter of slaughterhouse workers are ill or injured at any one time. Human Rights Watch referred to their job as the most dangerous in the country.

Human deaths are not uncommon in slaughterhouses, though they are of course far less common than those of non-human animals. Slaughter lines are constantly being made faster for the sake of profit, at the risk of those wielding sharp and dangerous weapons. The ASPCA (American Society for the Prevention of Cruelty to Animals) found that this also means that animals are more likely to be slaughtered while fully conscious, after being ineffectively stunned.

Sadly, it's not uncommon to hear about the deaths of people who work at slaughterhouses. Nobody deserves to be put in unsafe conditions, or to die, at their workplace.

Across the United States, Australia, Germany and Brazil, the COVID-19 pandemic showed us that injuries aren't the only danger to slaughterhouse workers. Slaughterhouses caused major COVID-19 outbreaks and saw disproportionate infections among workers. This is largely due to the high-speed kill lines and shoulder-to-shoulder working environments. It's also because corporations that run slaughterhouses are, as one 2019 article wrote, 'treating workers like meat'.

The poor treatment of slaughterhouse workers

When we talk about someone being treated like meat, we mean that we dehumanise them, we objectify them, we treat them as though they don't have thoughts or feelings. Perhaps the reason workers are so often mistreated in this industry is because animal bodies and lives are not valued in it, making way for and normalising a lack of value for any life – including those of humans.

An Oxfam report showed that slaughterhouse workers across America sometimes wear diapers because they are denied toilet breaks. This is not how people ought to be treated.

It gets worse. Despite false ally claims of 'multiculturalism at its best', migrants and refugees in Australian slaughterhouses have been reported to be underpaid, and get put into inadequate, overcrowded rental accommodation.

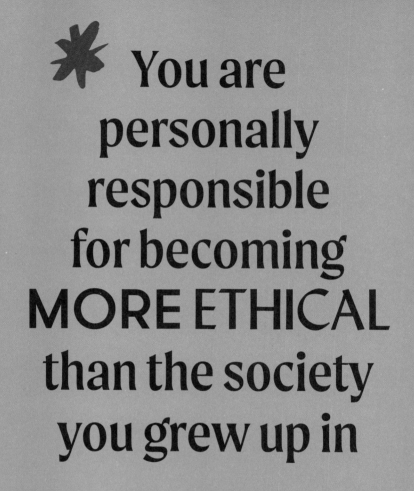

You are personally responsible for becoming MORE ETHICAL than the society you grew up in

Eliezer Yudkowsky

The mental implications of slaughterhouse work

Please note that the following section may be distressing, and references serious mental health struggles and suicide. Please know there is support if these themes distress you.

Most people have heard of post-traumatic stress disorder (PTSD). It's a serious mental condition which haunts people who have witnessed or experienced a traumatic event. Fewer people have heard of perpetration-induced stress disorder (PITS). It's a similar condition, with a fundamental difference – the trauma comes not from having experienced trauma yourself, but from being 'the direct reason for another being's trauma', according to the Yale Global Health Review.

The symptoms of PITS are similar to those of PTSD, including 'drug and alcohol abuse, anxiety, panic, depression, increased paranoia, a sense of disintegration, dissociation or amnesia, which are incorporated into the "psychological consequences" of the act of killing'. Both soldiers and slaughterhouse workers experience the devastating impact of PITS.

Imagine you were made to kill a dog. You had to look into their pleading eyes, and shoot them in the head anyway. You had to slice across their throat as they bled. Imagine how horrific this experience would be for you. Imagine the animal wasn't a dog, but a pig, or a cow who looked up at you before you did this. The horror wouldn't go away.

The mental impact of slaughtering can, unfortunately, lead to thoughts of suicide or the act itself. A harrowing recount of life in a slaughterhouse was once shared on the BBC, with the worker stating, 'I personally suffered from depression, a condition exacerbated by the long hours, the relentless work, and being surrounded by death. After a while, I started feeling suicidal.' This person shares that one of his co-workers often made jokes about 'not being here in six months', and one day that he broke down, sobbing as he shared his suicidal thoughts. A few months after the depressed slaughterhouse worker finally left his job, unable to cope any longer, he heard that his co-worker had killed himself.

The impact of slaughtering on human communities

Like a kettle boiling over, the harm that is done to animals, which harms the humans causing it, also hurts the communities these humans live in. In other words, there are serious dangers to living in the areas surrounding slaughterhouses.

A study published in *Organization and Environment* shows us that across 500 US counties, communities surrounding slaughterhouses fall victim to disproportionately high numbers of violent offences, including sexual assault and rape. Paid to act violently towards animal individuals, this study refers to the violence toward human communities by slaughterhouse workers as 'spillover in the psyches' of these people. Violence is violence, and this job is not one that allows for any kind of respect for autonomy, consent, or safety of bodies that are different to our own, that are considered 'less than'.

When I spoke to undercover animal cruelty investigator Rich Hardy, he told me that his work, and being so constantly confronted and surrounded by violence towards animals, had made him realise that 'we are all capable of becoming immune to cruelties and injustices if we are exposed to them for long enough'. These forms of horrific violence and violation that slaughterhouse workers commit against the humans in their communities are never excusable or justified by their being traumatised. However, it is critical we understand the root of these problems if we ever hope to fix them. The root of the problem is any normalised, industrialised violence.

Farming animals: the mental impact

If we go back a step further in the supply chains that bring us animal-derived foods and fashion, we meet farmers. Unlike slaughterhouse workers, who don't know the animals they kill before there's no life left to know, farmers often feel a connection to the animals they raise. Feeling a connection to animals you know you have to get killed in order to make a living isn't easy.

In the award-winning short film *73 Cows*, we meet Jay and his wife, Katja. They farm cattle who are killed so that people can eat them and wear them. In the film, Jay and Katja's efforts to move to veganic (vegan organic) farming with the help of The Vegan Society were documented, as were their efforts to provide a forever home for the seventy-three remaining cows they couldn't bear to kill.

Jay is a soft man. In an interview, he shared that he stopped eating animals he had 'known and cared for' over two decades before he stopped sending them to slaughter. He described feeling trapped in the work that was handed down to him from his father.

'You couldn't help thinking, "Do they know what you really have in store for them?" and wondering if they knew that you would betray their trust in you.' Jay felt he had to 'steel himself' to send cows to slaughter, feeling like a 'criminal playing a dirty horrible trick' on those animals. Near the end of the film, among beautiful scenes of frolicking free cows at a sanctuary and a smiling Jay, Katja speaks to how the transition away from raising animals for slaughter has impacted the man she loves. 'I think the biggest change is, I think that he talks more ... that is just so beautiful to see.'

PERSPECTIVE

Those who've worked in slaughterhouses

I have spoken to a few ex-slaughterhouse workers. The first, who came up to me at a demonstration, told me that he eventually quit his work because of the nightmares. This man was agitated and skittish. He pointed at a screen where activists were playing footage of standard practices in slaughterhouses, and told me he 'used to do that stuff', and that he started seeing it every night when he went to sleep, killing animal after animal as they each fought to live, crying out in fear. The only difference between his waking hours and those spent in his nightmares was that the animals he killed when he dreamed had cries that sounded like human children.

The second slaughterhouse worker I spoke to was someone called Craig. Craig spoke of moving from mopping blood-caked floors to feeling it gush out of the throats of animals he'd just taken life from. But it wasn't only the beating of animals he saw, or their lifeless eyes looking back at him that he spoke about, it was the culture within the slaughterhouse, too.

Craig said that there were a lot of drugs used in slaughterhouses. He, and most people around him, used them to cope – with the trauma, and with the physical pain and exhaustion. He told me that any women he had seen working there were harassed, that any concerned feelings about animals expressed were seen as shameful. He told me some of the people he was closer to at the slaughterhouse were refugees who had fled violence, only to end up covered in blood every day. He also told me how much better he felt now that he didn't work in a slaughterhouse. There is a way forward for everyone, and we need to support those who want out.

Toxic masculinity and meat (and leather, dairy, eggs, and so on)

Jay steeled himself as he directed the cows he cared for onto a truck heading somewhere they wouldn't return from. Craig kept quiet in the slaughterhouse about how traumatic it was when he first killed an animal because he knew he would be 'picked on and bullied' by older men. Advertisements like '100% manly man, 100% pure beef' make out that you can't be a real man if you don't eat flesh. Some men seem to think that if you can't or won't hunt and shoot an animal, you should hand in your 'man card'. What is happening here? Why should what you eat have anything to do with your gender or expression of? Well, toxic masculinity is what's happening here.

There's obviously nothing wrong with being a man, and there's nothing wrong with masculinity, but there is plenty wrong with patriarchal ideas of masculinity that have become toxified and skewed: that shames the expression of vulnerability, tenderness and emotion. Today, too many men tie masculinity to their ability to dominate, to be powerful, and so to violate. This is where feminism and veganism start to intertwine.

*It is SOUL DESTROYING

Ex-cattle farmer
Jay Wilde

# EXPLAINER

What's feminism got to do with veganism?

Carol J Adams wrote *The Sexual Politics of Meat* back in 1990, and the messages inside this book still need to be talked about today. Adams describes animals as 'absent referents' in their own consumption. They, or their flesh, have taken on metaphorical meaning while we continue to look away from animals themselves.

Women face a crisis of gender-based violence which sees them more likely to be killed by their male partners than anyone else, to be raped, to be sexually assaulted, tormented and stalked. As a result, sometimes women describe themselves as having been made to feel 'like a piece of meat'. We as women reference 'meat' because the butchered bodies of animals have been made to represent the highest form of disenfranchisement, of objectification. Of course, just as we women are not 'just' pieces of meat, nor is the meat itself. Meat is flesh, a carcass, a body; 'meat' is an animal.

In the dairy and egg industries especially, we treat female animals as objects to exploit for their sexual organs. Dairy cows are forcibly impregnated and have their young taken from them so we can consume their milk instead, over and over until they are slaughtered. Egg-laying hens are exhausted by a constant and unnatural cycle of laying which ends when their ovaries are considered worthless, and then they too are killed. We deny these feminine animals their autonomy, we don't seek their consent, we ignore their attempts to free themselves.

No one is consumable, no one is an object. When we see someone as such, it's a slippery slope towards the objectification of others.

Why the far right are obsessed with soy

Toxic masculinity is wielded as a tool by far-right politicians who claim more liberal people, the left, are trying to destroy manhood. Harry Styles wearing a dress on the cover of Vogue was even called 'an outright attack' on traditional values that supposedly keep the world spinning. (He looked fantastic, by the way.) The term 'soy boy' is increasingly being used in far-right circles because men who drink soy milk, who don't support the violent dairy industry or environmental destruction are apparently effeminate. And, obviously, femininity is bad.

'They want to take your hamburgers' was proclaimed by former White House aide Sebastian Gorka, referring to the Green New Deal. Mike Pence, when opposing Kamala Harris' announcement that she would change American dietary guidelines to have a reduced amount of red meat for environmental and health reasons, said that he's 'got some red meat' for her.

This obsession with meat is an obsession with an outdated idea of masculinity, with superiority, with dominance, with the violence it allows for, that it normalises against humans, too.

# EXPLAINER

Class issues and animal consumption

Wealthy conservatives have loved their meat for a long time. In the Romantic Era of the 19th century, more people began to avoid eating foods that came from or were made of animals. This wasn't only because of a concern for the other species on this planet, but because of a rising class consciousness. The theory behind vegetarianism – which in that period was the term used to describe what we now call veganism – and animal liberation had started to intersect more obviously with other social justice movements as people came to understand the inefficiencies of animal agriculture. It was in this era that abolitionist and author Thomas Day referred to eating animals as a means to 'gratify a guilty sensuality'. A wider movement of people saw that it was a greedy vice of the wealthy who could afford to eat meat regularly, at the expense of everyone else.

This makes sense. As we know, plant-based food requires far less land than animal-derived foods, so to waste land that could be growing plants for direct human consumption, and to waste resources and labour on producing meals that are more expensive (without current subsidies that skew all of this) and available to less people, is classist.

The animal consumption of the ruling class, of those with privilege, was once seen as symbolic of oppression and consumerism. It still should be. So many people starve today while factory farms full of animals are stuffed with food that is often flown across the world to feed them. These animals are fattened to be meals for those who can afford their flesh. There is something very wrong and very unjust about our system.

Today,
820 MILLION
people do not have
enough food to EAT

WHO

Each year,
we feed over 70
**BILLION FARMED
ANIMALS** on land

FAO

Chapter Four

HOW VEGANISM *Helps* HEALTH

Evolution and meat

We've all heard the whole, 'Cavemen ate meat, so why shouldn't I?' argument. In what we often think of as 'caveman times', times I am glad not to live in for a whole array of reasons, but which people opposed to veganism seem to crave the replication of, yes, we killed, ate and wore animals. Cavemen also did a whole lot of things that we don't think are right anymore.

We do a lot of things today that we didn't used to. We wear clothing that has zippers on it, we use computers, we have mattresses, we stream music and movies, and speak to people on the other side of the world with the touch of a button. We've changed a lot since we first became 'human' on Earth, and whether we do something now, or did something back then, should not influence what we should be doing in the future.

In any case, archaeological findings suggest that prehistoric humans actually mostly ate vegetables. There's no denying they ate meat, too, but it wasn't the centrepiece of every meal. It's often thought not only that meat was most of what our way back ancestors ate, but that eating meat is what made us smart. This claim doesn't have that much logic behind it either.

A lot of research, including the work of Yuval Noah Harari in his book *Sapiens*, suggests it is far more likely that it was our ability to control and cook with fire that helped grow our brains. When we developed this skill, many hundreds of thousands of years ago, suddenly what we could eat became a lot more varied. Wheat, rice and potatoes were all foods that were inedible until this moment. Suddenly, they were staples – and they still are.

Chimpanzees spend up to seven hours a day chewing raw food, whereas humans spend only one hour a day eating cooked food. The cooked food that we eat is easier to digest because it's easier to chew, and it's softer, whether that food be a starchy plant, a fruit, a vegetable or a piece of flesh. Over time, our teeth became smaller as they chewed more easily, and our intestines became shorter as they processed what we put into them more quickly. Ultimately, this meant less energy spent digesting, fuelling ourselves and surviving, and more energy to spend thinking and developing. As time went on, we continued to develop, often without scientific understanding to explain it. However, what we do know is that the age of enlightenment had nothing to do with diet change.

Basically, don't worry – you can still be a genius if you're a vegan.

Cancer and animal foods

Not only can cancer devastate the health of tannery workers and people living near factory farms, it can also sicken people who eat animals. While, without data supporting them, the meat industry continues to cry out that vegan meat alternatives are against nature and bad for us, the WHO has classified the eating of kinds of animal-derived foods as carcinogenic or as probable carcinogens – causing or likely causing cancer.

Below is a table outlining which kinds of animal-derived foods are categorised as such, and what other carcinogens are grouped alongside them.

Group	Group meaning	Animal-derived food	Others in group
Group 1: Human carcinogens	Sufficient, convincing evidence that agents cause cancer in humans.	Processed meats – including those that are cured, smoked, salted. Sausages, ham, corned beef, some salted fish, beef jerky, meat-based preparations and sauces.	Leather dust, neutron radiation, plutonium, tobacco, asbestos.
Group 2A: Probably carcinogenic to humans	'A positive association has been observed between exposure to the agent and cancer ... other explanations for the observations (technically termed chance, bias, or confounding) could not be ruled out.'	Red meats, including the flesh of all mammals. These are labelled as beef, lamb, veal, pork and so on. Meat from goats, kangaroos, moose and other mammals are included.	Methyl methanesulfonate, glyphosate, inorganic lead compounds, hydrazine. These are not necessarily equally probable carcinogens to humans, but all probably cause cancer.

The kinds of cancers caused by eating this animal flesh are varied. Eating mammals is a probable cause of colorectal or bowel cancer, pancreatic cancer and prostate cancer.

Five years after diagnosis of pancreatic cancer, John Hopkins Medicine states that only five to ten per cent of people are alive. The American Society of Clinical Oncology reports that bowel cancer has a five-year survival rate of 63 per cent, but if the cancer is diagnosed before it spreads, that jumps up to a more hopeful

90 per cent. Fortunately, the five-year survival rate for localised prostate cancer is nearly 100 per cent, but if it has not been caught quickly – as can sometimes happen – the survival rate is 31 per cent. Processed meat is known to cause colorectal cancer, and an inconclusive association to stomach cancer exists too.

How serious is the link between meat and cancer? How much do you need to be eating for it to have an impact? The WHO states that 'an analysis of data from ten studies estimated that every 50-gram portion of processed meat eaten daily increases the risk of bowel cancer by about 18 per cent'.

There's more. There are also growing bodies of evidence, addressed in the study titled 'Dietary Patterns and Breast Cancer Risk: A Study in 2 Cohorts', that sticking to a plant-based diet may protect against breast cancer, too. Interestingly, plant-based diets have been shown not only to reduce the risk of cancer, but even to slow the progress of it in some cases. A plant-based diet has been shown to be therapeutic, and even able to decrease the rate of disease progression for people with prostate cancer, as shown in peer-reviewed studies 'Are Strict Vegetarians [Vegans] Protected Against Prostate Cancer?' and 'Adoption of a Plant-Based Diet by patients with Recurrent Prostate Cancer'. As we continue to learn so much more about cancer, as disease that was once seen as an almost certain death sentence for everyone afflicted by it, there continues to be more hope.

Other health issues associated with consuming land-dwelling animals, fish, dairy and eggs

Cancer is not the only risk associated with eating animal-derived foods. It's perhaps not even the most substantial. Dr Mehr Gupta, with the help of a large amount of high-quality evidence from countless studies, talked me through what else there is to know about health and eating the bodies of animals.

Cardiovascular disease is the cause of an enormous amount of sickness and death in our society, and so the benefits of reducing it are obviously enormous, too. Cardiovascular disease (CVD) includes heart attacks and strokes, and includes risk factors like high cholesterol, high blood pressure and diabetes. Numerous studies have shown that the development of plaque in blood vessels, which can impact blood supply to the heart and brains, which leads to CVD, can be caused by a diet containing high levels of saturated fats, like dairy and red meat in particular. Plant-based diets have been proven to lower blood pressure and cholesterol, and even induce remission in non-insulin dependent diabetes. They can reduce the amount of plaque in people's blood vessels, and their risk of future heart attacks. That's pretty huge.

Even health conditions like dementia are increasingly being tied to the food we eat, and our guts. One of my grandmothers died with dementia, and I know just how frightening, confusing and upsetting this disease is. What I didn't know then is that in 2013, a year earlier, the International Conference on Nutrition and the Brain saw experts recommend a diet that included vegetables, legumes like beans, peas and lentils, fruits and whole grains, instead of meats and dairy, in order to prevent dementia.

Chronic kidney disease, as well as rheumatoid arthritis, and the chronic respiratory condition, asthma, all have potential links to the consumption of animal-based foods too, and all have studies which suggest a plant-based diet may be able to assist with symptoms.

While this has all mostly been about meat and dairy, there's more to consider. Let's talk about fish. Considered a 'brain food' by many, fish contains mercury, sometimes in dangerous levels. Mercury can cause brain damage at levels that are extreme, which is concerning, considering that one study in the journal *Environmental Toxicology and Chemistry* found that studies of mercury levels in 'three national brands of canned tuna ... 55 per cent of the tuna examined was above the US Environmental Protection Agency's safety level for human consumption'. In addition, as we continue to pollute the planet with plastic, this has an impact on our oceanic friends, and on us, if we choose to cut that positive relationship by eating them. A UN report shared that there are more than 51 trillion microscopic plastic particles in the sea, 'more than 500 times the number of stars in the Milky Way'. A regular portion of mussels from Europe could contain about ninety microplastic pieces. Microplastics have been found in fish, including in canned fish, and even in sea salt.

Finally, in the case of eggs, you might be interested to know that the American Egg Board has been disallowed by the United States Department of Agriculture from referring to eggs as 'healthy' and 'nutritious' in their advertisements due to their high level of saturated fat and cholesterol, which again, is tied to cardiovascular disease, and potentially even dementia. This was discovered by Dr Michael Greger after he was granted relevant documents through the Freedom of Information Act.

Intolerance and dietary racism

Did you know that 90 per cent of Asian communities are intolerant to lactose? And so are 75 per cent of African American people, according to data analysed by the Physicians Committee for Responsible Medicine. Despite this, FAO describes Asia as the strongest growing region for dairy consumption, and US Dietary Guidelines encourage Black Americans to consume dairy regularly – as most dietary guidelines do.

While at first this might seem accidentally harmful – caused by a lack of awareness, slow updating of guidelines, or something else – many people criticise governments of something more sinister. Prominent Black physician Dr Milton Mills calls current dietary guidelines 'an egregious form of institutional racism'. In fact, he's addressed the advisory committee in charge of these guidelines to critique this issue, and has researched and reported on racial bias in nutrition policy.

Lobbyists from all animal agricultural industries, including dairy, are paid a large amount of money to ensure their foods are encouraged to be eaten. 'To intentionally harm the health of a large swath of our population so that industry operatives can profit from it', Dr Mills says, is 'reprehensible'. Dr Mills speaks to this issue in the Black-created film, *The Invisible Vegan*. In this film, lauren T Ornelas of the Food Empowerment Project speaks about food and injustice too, with a focus on food deserts. A food desert is an area with less access to supermarkets full of fresh, healthy foods, so people must travel to get these. Often, if healthy foods are available for purchase in these areas, they're too expensive for people to regularly consume. These kinds of inaccessibility issues overwhelmingly impact communities of colour, particularly Black communities, making food deserts a form of environmental racism. Food security is out of reach for many Aboriginal and Torres Strait Islander peoples in Australia too.

In the documentary *They're Trying To Kill Us*, it's claimed that this is all 'by design', a covert and systemic form of racism which further perpetuates a kind of segregation, worsening the opportunities for these people to build themselves up the way white people are given the resources to. This is another kind of racism, caused by false ideas of supremacy and another kind of intolerance. This is dietary racism.

Myth-busting: veganism, health and wellness

MYTH

Eating soy will mess with my hormone levels.

No, it won't. Everything in the world is made up of chemicals. Inside of us, we have oestrogen. Inside of soy, there is phytoestrogen. These aren't the same things. These chemicals can bind to our oestrogen receptors, but they don't act the same way oestrogen does – so they won't cause you to grow breasts if you don't have any, or anything like that. Phytoestrogen actually has antioxidant and anti-inflammatory properties. Some people have pointed out that if soy milk, soy sauce, or soy-based meat alternatives really could help people grow larger breasts, they'd be in much higher demand!

MYTH

You need to take a B12 supplement as a vegan, so it must be an unhealthy way of living!

It's true that vegans should take a B12 supplement or eat foods fortified with B12 (like a lot of plant milks are). But here's what you might not know: B12 isn't something that is exclusive to animals. B12 is a vitamin, and certain bacteria help to create it. These bacteria are found in soil, algae and even some plant sources. Animals eating grass and bits of soil will often benefit from the vitamin. While people who eat animals will get B12 from this, many people don't realise that farmed animals are often fed or injected with a B12 supplement. We can supplement B12 far more directly by taking it ourselves. Additional fun fact: research from the Harvard School of Public Health has found that based on genetics – not diet – 40 per cent of people in the US may be deficient in this vitamin.

MYTH

My bones will get weak without the calcium from dairy.

No, they won't. Milk is a source of calcium, there's no argument to that. However, it's also designed to be full of fats and hormones that help a baby calf grow into a full-sized cow. We don't need milk anymore once we've stopped drinking breast milk (cow's milk is for baby cows like human's milk is for baby humans). Plant-based sources of calcium are protective of bones, and don't carry the risk of chronic disease that dairy products like milk, cheese and yoghurt do. Overall, risks of fractures or osteoporosis with healthy plant-based diets are low, as shown by peer-reviewed studies like 'Veganism and Osteoporosis: A Review of the Current Literature', which validates what healthy vegans walking around already experience.

MYTH

I won't be able to have any muscle or play sports well.

You'll be able to have muscle, and play sports well if you want to. In the documentary *The Game Changers*, plant-based athletes including world record-holding strongman Patrik Baboumian, Kendrick Farris, the American record-holding weightlifter, record-holding ultramarathon runner Scott Jurek, two-time Australian running champ Morgan Mitchell, and eight-time US national cycling champion Dotsie Bausch crush this myth. There's no science behind claims that people eating plant-based foods are at a disadvantage. There is, however, evidence that eating plant-based foods can improve vascular flow to muscles and decrease inflammation in the body, while increasing glycogen storage.

MYTH

Eating vegan in a healthy way is expensive. It's a privilege for the few.

Eating vegan is expensive only if you acquire a more expensive taste. Just like making a lentil and bean bolognese is cheaper than making one from beef, it will be cheaper than making one from vegan mince. Canned and tinned foods, seasonal, local vegetables are all more affordable than meat and dairy as long as you're living somewhere where these foods are accessible – and chances are, you will be. Are you personally able to be vegan? We need to use our privilege to ensure we are protecting the planet, our communal health and the safety of animals, for those who genuinely aren't able to right now.

 **ACTION**

Learn from the work of vegans of colour

We know that veganism isn't a white thing, but it's often still presented that way. This isn't reflective of the vegan movement or population, but an issue of representation. Aph Ko said to the New York Times that 'the Black vegan movement is one of the most diverse, decolonial, complex and creative movements'. As well as writing books on feminism, Black veganism and liberation, Ko is the creator of Black Vegans Rock, which highlights, you guessed it, Black vegans doing important work in the movement. Many of these people focus on access to healthy food, food justice and Black health as a form of political resistance to racism. Here's a list of some Black and Brown people to follow:

✳ **Amie Breeze Harper PhD** is a scholar, public speaker and the author of *Sistah Vegan: Black Female Vegans Speak on Food, Identity, Health and Society*.

✳ **Tracye McQuirter** is an award-winning public health nutritionist, best-selling author and the creator of *By Any Greens Necessary*.

✳ **lauren T Ornelas** is the founder and president of Food Empowerment Project which looks at and addresses food and dietary inequality, as well as farm worker rights.

✳ **Monique Koch** is the creator of Brown Vegan. She is a public speaker, blogger and cook who helps people live vegan in a simple way. Her podcast discusses diet culture, community building and more, with other, mostly Black vegan women as guests.

* **Debbie Morales** is known on Instagram as @sisoyvegan, and she shares recipes alongside information about environmentalism, racism, food accessibility and intersectional veganism.

* **Tabitha Brown**, coined the world's favourite Mom, is joy personified, and shares videos about vegan food and cooking.

* **Zipporah**, known as @zipporahthevegan on Instagram is a pro-Black, anti-diet vegan who shares content on veganism, anti-racism, food and more. Zipporah also talks about her experience with veganism and a past eating disorder.

Case study: The politician who took on public health in a new way

Eric Adams is the Mayor of New York City, and he's the second Black person to hold the position. With a large Black and Brown population, this kind of reflective leadership, which stands for the protection of a marginalised, oppressed, yet innovative, resilient and vibrant community, is critical.

He told me that he once followed a common 'junky' American diet, had Type 2 diabetes, vision loss, and nerve damage in his hands and feet. He had high blood pressure and cholesterol, and an ulcer. He decided to make a change. Within three weeks of eating a wholefood, plant-based diet, his vision came back. Within three months, his body became healthy again; his diabetes going into remission, his ulcer and nerve damage disappearing, and his blood and cholesterol levels returning to a healthy state.

Today, Adams holds the belief that 'you can't abuse living beings and expect for it not to abuse you in the process', as we 'come from the same core' so must 'determine how we are going to take care of ourselves and our mothers', and also 'of Mother Earth'. Wanting to show his community that they could be more in control of their health, and not need a lifetime of medicine in many cases, Adams has set himself a mission to foster a more mentally and physically healthy community.

This is an important goal, because as reported by Cigna, Black communities in America experience significant disparities in chronic conditions, access to mental and physical health care, and preventative screenings. Adams has stood up against a lack of government action and worked to set up initiatives regarding extremely high suicide rates among Black youth. He has, despite the requests for retraction by The North American Meat Institute, set up Meatless Mondays at New York public schools, and successfully seen the Department of Education effectively ban carcinogenic processed meats from being served in these schools.

What's more, as part of New York's Green New Deal, which tackles the city's climate footprint, Adams led the 'green action' against processed meat and beef, with not only schools, but hospitals, prisons and municipal offices committing to reduce their beef purchases by 50 per cent. He has also worked with forty doctors of colour to promote the health benefits of wholefood plant-based diets, especially as people of colour were dying at higher rates of COVID-19 due to pre-existing conditions. Hoping it will extend across further hospitals, Adams has set up a pilot lifestyle medicine clinic in the oldest hospital in America, Bellevue. This clinic, with the help of doctors, nurses, dieticians and coaches, will work with patients to educate and change their eating patterns, helping communities prevent and even reverse diet-related health issues.

Collective health

It is deeply important that when we consider the health benefits of eating vegan and of transitioning to a plant-based agricultural system, we consider marginalised individuals. Not only are poorer Black, Indigenous and other people of colour more likely to experience environmental racism or to work in dangerous jobs in the animal industrial complex, they are more likely to suffer from the personal health problems discussed here. Significant documented disparities in cardiovascular health, cancer deaths, and other health crises across different races and ethnicities are well documented. Poorer people have less access to the healthcare that they deserve to stay safe when they do become sick. Advocating for healthier food benefits ourselves as individuals, but also as a collective. This is why access to these healthy, plant-based foods is so important.

There are real costs to animal agriculture that are invisible today. These include the economic burden forced upon sick people and our healthcare system, which is almost always struggling to cope – because of a lack of funding, a lack of staff, a lack of resources.

A study from Oxford University found that if by 2050 we had all switched to a plant-based diet, the decrease in health risks associated with animal-derived foods would result in economic benefits of, at the very least, USD\$1 trillion globally, every single year. This kind of money could be invested into ensuring everyone has access to a safe home, to education, to a good life. It could be invested into renewable energy, into the protection of climate refugees, or a vast number of other important things.

Another fun fact: this same plant-based switch could also afford us all a cumulative 129 million years of life saved!

Zoonotic disease

While we're already acutely aware of the risks zoonotic diseases bring us – COVID-19 being one of them – we may not realise quite how common they are, and how much our current system exacerbates the risk of their rise.

The WHO reports that zoonotic diseases – those transmitted from animals to humans – make up 75 per cent of all new emerging infectious diseases. COVID-19 is certainly not the first animal-origin virus to infect humans. The avian bird flu came from factory-farmed chickens, swine flu came from factory-farmed pigs, both have killed thousands of people, and come from the keeping of animals in horrific, confined conditions. WHO also documents that the 1918 influenza pandemic, which killed at least 50 million people, was zoonotic, as are the vast majority of pandemic influenzas. Since the rise of COVID-19, fur factory farms across the world have closed down as the disease spread to mink. The wildlife trade and exotic skin trade have been defined as risky to our societal health. Pig and chicken factory farms globally continue to spit out new strains and cases of dangerous zoonotic disease.

If we left animals in peace and ate and wore plants instead, we would all be safer.

Antibiotic resistance

It's not just zoonotic diseases. We also need to talk about antibiotic resistance, and the potential reality of a post-antibiotics world.

The first man to receive antibiotics accidentally scratched his face with a rose thorn as he walked into his garden. Before he was given penicillin, then a new and experimental drug, his whole face swelled up, his eye needed to be removed while his abscesses needed draining, and his other eye was continually pricked to calm swelling and pain. Days after receiving these antibiotics, he was recovering, but when there wasn't enough of the medication available yet to complete his recovery, he died.

This was the world before antibiotics. A time where small cuts and injuries could be a death sentence. Today, we rely on antibiotics to have surgery and dental work safely, to protect us from sexually transmitted infections, minor cuts that go bad, and a whole lot of other, fairly everyday things.

Today, some sexually transmitted infections, as well as infections like tuberculosis and pneumonia are becoming harder to treat because antibiotics are becoming less effective. It's well recognised that more infections will become resistant to antibiotics, rendering them useless, because the more we use antibiotics, the more the pathogens attacking us 'learn' to resist them. This is why your doctor isn't supposed to prescribe you antibiotics unless you really need them. The WHO describes this problem as one of the biggest threats to global health today.

Princeton University and WHO literature shares that a shocking 73 per cent of antibiotics used around the world are tied to animal agriculture, where they are fed to prevent sickness in cramped, cruel, illness-inducing conditions. It's cheaper to feed farmed animals antibiotics than to actually care for their needs, so we waste antibiotics by feeding them straight to these animals who deserve to be freed from the conditions they are forced to live in. Sometimes, as is noted in the *American Journal of Public Health*, antibiotics are used simply to fatten animals up faster for their slaughter.

With such heavy-handed use of antibiotics, bacteria that are resistant to them are becoming more and more commonplace, with resistance seen in farmed animals nearly tripling since 2000. These disease-causing antibiotic-resistant bacteria can be transmitted to humans not only through direct contact, but through eating these animals.

If we want to keep the medical miracles we have created, we need to change the way we view animals.

✱ More affluent people today eat far more meat than our PREHISTORIC ancestors did. It doesn't give them SUPERPOWERS, but it does increase their likelihood of some cancers, and other diseases

Part Three

SAVING ANIMALS

Chapter Five

Animal Life

Are you someone, or have you ever met someone, who is just so incredibly in love with an animal? I'm like that with my dog, Bella. She's been with me since I was about nine years old, and she still lives with me today. The most beloved people in my life know that the individual who can make me feel better more than anyone else is Bella. She has seen me through some of my toughest times, and it doesn't matter that we can't share a verbal language. We share so many forms of affection and a very strong non-verbal language. I know when she wants food, play or security from me, and she knows when I need comfort from her. I love this dog a ridiculous amount.

You know who else I love like that? Willow, the first orphaned lamb I ever fostered. She was just a couple of days old when I began caring for her. It was so special to watch her personality grow. Night after night of cuddles and warm bottles of milk, I watched her become more confident. More playful. More sure of herself as she was able to grow and thrive in a space that was safe. Willow is a grown-up sheep now and I still love and care for her the same way. Knowing that she is protected, happy and free is so wonderful, but it's also bittersweet because I know that she, and the other animals in her sanctuary home, like chickens, turkeys, cows, goats and pigs, are the very lucky few. I know that for each of those animals, who I know by name, who have favourite head scratch spots, favourite pastimes and favourite friends, there are countless more who are subjected to intense cruelty, who are slaughtered before they can even become their fully grown selves.

These sanctuary-dwelling animals, like Willow, or Atlas the goat, saved from a dairy where he would have been killed as a newborn, are reminders of every individual who never got a chance at safety.

Well over 2,300 individual, land-dwelling animals are slaughtered every second, according to UN FAO data. In the time it took for you to read that sentence, about 9,200 were killed.

It is phenomenally difficult to imagine the scale of such suffering. If you enjoy the company of a companion dog or cat, try to imagine their fear and suffering if they were in this position. Try to multiply that suffering thousands of times.

# ✳ EXPLAINER

Speciesism

Speciesism refers to the belief that human beings are superior to other animals. This belief is often used by humans as a justification for the exploitation of other animals. We can't talk about the animal industrial complex without talking about animals themselves. Specifically, non-human animals – remember, we are animals, too!

Discussions around the way we treat, see and objectify non-human animals are often very uncomfortable, and this is natural, considering that speciesism is something deeply ingrained in all of us. It can feel strange and unnerving to reassess the way we categorise others, how we treat them, and what they are really like. However, we must talk about non-humans, as their suffering is at the epicentre of everything we have looked at in this book. This industry thrives upon turning their bodies into commodities.

Speciesism is a form of discrimination like any other. These are all forms of oppression, and they all function in the same way: one group is falsely labelled as better than or superior to another, and this is used to deem acceptable horrific violence and injustice against the supposedly 'lesser' group. Essentially, oppression is a structure and different forms of discrimination are simply different symptoms of this same root.

In the case of human animals, there are many justifications for the false idea that we are superior to all other species – because we can speak, because we can create computers, because we are 'at the top of the food chain', because we are smart. All of these justifications are very human-centric and based on understandings of communication and intelligence that are relevant to us alone. It's the whole 'measure the intelligence of a fish by their ability to climb a tree' problem.

Regardless, other species do communicate with each other and are intelligent too. While they may not be able to build computers (though, I can't personally do that either), they can do plenty of other things. Some species are able to fairly share resources among their communities in ways we humans are often yet to master. Some can swim fast, or climb amazing heights, and even use echolocation to understand their surroundings. Many take great care for the environment they live in, and do all sorts of different, unique-to-their-species things. In any case, intelligence is a bad marker of who should be treated with dignity and respect.

Just in the same way that we are not better or worse based on our race, gender, sexual orientation, age or other factor, animals are not better or worse than each other – including ourselves. We are all simply different. And difference, as we're so often taught from childhood, is not a justification for treating someone poorly. It's certainly no justification for mass violence and slaughter.

Speciesism is so deeply entrenched in our society that not only are animals outside of humanity considered lesser, they're barely considered to be individuals. Animals are commodified, called 'stock' who happen to be alive, transformed into snacks and stilettos. Speciesism is the root justification for every atrocity that is done upon other species on this planet. So let's look closer at these atrocities, and how we frame them.

Animal welfare

The mainstream discussion of the treatment of animals – be they those we think of as pets, as food or as entertainers – is one about 'welfare'. Animal welfare discussions usually look at how cruelty and suffering can be reduced, while these animals can continue to be exploited to fill the purposes we've decided they solely exist for.

For example, the RSPCA are an animal welfare organisation. They talk about why it's important to treat farmed animals well, but they have no problem with animals being slaughtered. This is not an uncommon perspective. It's kind of the ultimate betrayal – to recognise that animals are sentient, able to feel pain, fear and joy, and yet to render them 'food' and 'clothing'.

So how is animal welfare different from animal liberation? Animal liberation is about dismantling speciesism. It recognises that the species of an individual is not a justification for that individual to be objectified, incarcerated, mutilated, disenfranchised or killed. Just because a dog is not a human, does not mean we have the right to kill that dog, beat that dog, lock up that dog. Equally, the same can be said for pigs, or for chickens.

Animal welfare ideology, on the other hand, thinks that reducing animals to profitable commodities by owning and killing them is acceptable, so long as it is 'done well'. It's like a farm where there's only a small number of chickens, and three of them are called Lily, Milo and Nora. The three chickens have a lovely life, get to peck bugs out of the grass, feel the sunshine and dust bathe before getting head pats from the farmer as they purr (chickens purr in relaxation!). When they're about a month old, Lily, Milo and Nora lose those comforts, their friendship, and everything, because they're killed so someone can eat them. It's done quickly. This is the 'animal welfare' approach to what animals like Lily, Milo and Nora are owed.

If this doesn't sit quite right with you, you might sit on the speciesism side of the fence.

As a society, we don't humour the idea that there is an acceptable way to kill another human being because they want to live, because it is not our right to take someone else's life. We wouldn't accept this idea for the beloved companion animals in our lives either. So why can chickens, fish, cattle and turkeys be 'humanely killed'?

Sentience and individuality

Sentience refers to an animal's ability to experience feelings. To feel is to be conscious, to respond to what is happening around you, to be aware.

In 2012 (better late than never), the Cambridge Declaration on Consciousness, written by 'a prominent international group of cognitive neuroscientists, neuropharmacologists, neurophysiologists, neuroanatomists and computational neuroscientists' declared that 'humans are not unique in possessing the neurological substrates that generate consciousness'.

A lot of the time, arguments about why we shouldn't kill animals sound something like, 'Pigs are as smart as dogs, if not smarter', or 'Pigs are as smart as three-year-old human children!' These comparisons frame pigs as worthy of very basic safeties and rights only because of their proximity to species we arbitrarily choose to value more highly, or to ourselves. They also frame intellect as a worthy indicator of who deserves what. Both of these things are dangerous.

The only thing that matters – whether someone is a human, a dog, a pig, a fish, a cat, an elephant, a duck, or a polar bear – is 'Does this individual feel?' We know that animals feel pain just as they feel pleasure. We know too, that many of them have close friends, that they have preferences, that they have fears as much as they have things that fill them with excitement. We all have lived experiences.

If we look again at animal sanctuaries, perhaps the most interesting thing about them is how different the animals there are. It can be easy to miss the individuality of animals like ducks, chickens, cattle and sheep because we think of them as homogenous collectives. As herds and groups that move as though with one mind, that do very little, that don't move too much, don't engage with us. At animal sanctuaries, the personalities of individuals come out – because they are in safe settings where their individuality is valued, where they are not seen as a resource, where they no longer need to fear violence.

These animals are full of life. Some enjoy cuddles, pats and affection. Some are boisterous, enjoying a bit of rough play. Some are more timid, and like to spend quality time with their most trusted animal companions, some are loud and demanding while others are gentle and patient.

It's not that animals who are farmed don't have personalities, it's that they are afraid of us, of our species, and what we do to them. Imagine a world where there was no need for such fear of us.

Including fish in our consideration

When we talk about animals, too often we forget about those who live underwater. It's not only dolphins, turtles or whales who are sea animals, but sharks, finned fish, crustaceans and so on. Just as the sentience of animals is forgotten too often, even the animality, so too the sentience of fish is forgotten.

Every year, at least one trillion fish are killed for our consumption, according to Fish Count. While that kind of number is impossible for us to grasp, we can at least recognise the suffering of one individual fish, and know that it is multiplied beyond our brain's own capacity to understand it. To do that though, we must first recognise that fish can suffer. And suffer they do. Fish respond positively to morphine pain relief, just like a human, which is interesting as morphine dulls the experience of pain, but does not cure the pain source itself. This means that pain is not only physical, but something that involves mental awareness.

Fish actively avoid that which has caused them pain in the past, and this is what causes 'hook-shyness', where some released fish who have been painfully caught on a hook stay far away from anything that looks like fishing gear, in fear of being captured and pierced into again.

Fish don't only feel physical pain, as is clearly shown through the work of leading behavioural ecologist Culum Brown among others, they also experience mental anguish. A Royal Society Open Science study found that one in four fish confined in bleak, underwater factory farms exhibit behaviours and brain chemistry that is nearly identical to that found in humans who are severely stressed and depressed. These depressed fish even have stunted growth and eat far less than those who are mentally healthier.

Crustaceans are sentient too. Crabs and lobsters have been found to learn and hold long-term memories around what is or is not a real threat to them. Some crabs also stand up for and protect their oceanic 'neighbours', but are picky about who they'll side with. Yet these animals are often boiled alive or frozen to death.

Even prawns, who have their eyes pulled off while conscious in some farms, and who are thought of as barely living by many, groom themselves when trying to treat pain on their antennae. Studies out of Queen's University Belfast have shown this is not just a reflex, but a response to pain.

With all of this in mind, we must see the confinement, mutilation and slaughter of fish species the same way we see the treatment of animals coated in fur or feathers. The bodies are different, and in fact the experiences are too, but they all involve pain, when these individuals can all feel positive emotions.

EXPLAINER

Carnism

Carnism is a specific expression of speciesism. It's a term coined by Dr Melanie Joy, author of *Why We Love Dogs, Eat Pigs and Wear Cows*, built upon Peter Singer's original discussion of speciesism. So what's the difference between them?

'Carn' means 'of the flesh', so carnism is specifically about the animals we eat. Speciesism sees us exploit dogs in puppy mills, lock up gorillas in zoos, perform cruel experiments on rabbits and lay out poison for rats, who we know from science show empathy, without a single care. Carnism is an 'invisible ideology' which centres around our food choices, and which sees most people choose to eat parts of dead animals. It is invisible because it is largely not thought of or named.

Carnism keeps us feeding on flesh through myth-making. These are the stories we are told about animals, and about meat. The centre of these myths is made up of the three n's, says Joy. We are told eating animals is *normal* because everyone does it. Yet, what is normal is changing all the time – it used to be normal for people to hit their children, but now it is mostly frowned upon and considered abuse – as it should be. We are also told that eating animals is necessary, which, by this point in the book, we've seen is not the case.

The final 'n' has a very strong hold on some of us: we are so often told that eating animals is natural, because we've done it forever. We consider what is natural to be wrong often though – the strong taking from the weak is what is natural, but we have chosen to try to function as a society that is more compassionate than that. In fact, the logical fallacy of appealing to nature is well documented, and something that is used to argue against vaccines and other lifesaving, modern medicine.

Natural isn't always best. But, to quote Remy from *Ratatouille* (another empathetic rat), I'd say that 'change *is* nature … the part that we can influence. And it all starts when we decide.'

Back to carnism and away from the little chef, let's talk about moral disengagement. This is where we choose to opt out of considering what we actually think is right, and instead avoid self-accountability. This plays a big part in carnism. We disengage from the problem of killing, eating and wearing sentient animals, by categorising animals as 'food animals', or 'livestock'. We remind ourselves that this is just how things are, we disconnect ourselves from the choice we are all able to make for ourselves, about what we think is acceptable and ethical.

To some people, moose and deer are 'food animals'. When I lived with my family in Sweden and ate these animals, I felt uncomfortable because I didn't agree with this categorisation. That was how I realised that 'food animals' didn't really exist; there are only animals, and our choice to kill, eat and wear them.

ACTION

Connect with the animals we are told are just food, clothing and test subjects

I could babble on about the theory behind how we see animals, and how our cultural norms misguide us into believing that some animals don't really feel that much emotion, don't really deserve their lives, don't really need freedom because they're 'lesser' than us. Or you could watch some cute videos, and get to know the animals we're talking about. (In fact, let's do both!)

Why not see if there's an animal sanctuary providing refuge and home to farmed animals who would otherwise be slaughtered, near you? Visit them! Learn about the individuals who live there, hear their stories, engage with them as individuals and see how your perception of animals of their species shifts. See how your perception of what we do to them shifts, too.

If there isn't a sanctuary near you, and even if there is, follow some sanctuaries online and do the same thing virtually. Some wonderful sanctuaries that have social media accounts include:

* Edgar's Mission
* Barn Sanctuary
* Farm Sanctuary
* Sisu Refuge
* Happily Heifer After Sanctuary
* Rancho Relaxo (Boo Chaces)
* Woodstock Farm Sanctuary

How marketing and language hides cruelty

Despite our farming systems being brutal and inhumane, we like to continue to imagine the picturesque farms of our dreams. It makes it easier for us to feel comfortable about eating individuals we tend to care for, at least to some extent.

Advertising and our own use of language play important roles in both maintaining this fantasy farm in our heads, and in diminishing the suffering of animals that we perceive. Multiple studies released by both the ASPCA and government bodies have shown that consumers across the US and Australia do not understand what all these labels mean, and assume better treatment of animals than what their purchases really pay for. It's not surprising, considering all the buzzwords and grassy meadow images we see every day.

Words like 'humane' are slapped onto packages of animal flesh to make us feel comfort, and to think there are consistent standards in place between farms with this label. Despite most American consumers assuming this to be true, there is generally no legal definition for the term 'humane'.

Across Europe, there is no harmonised system of animal-welfare labelling, so words like 'humane', 'high-welfare', 'free-range' and 'cage-free' may often mean something very different from what we suppose.

Eggs from 'happy hens' come from an industry which 'depopulates' hens, killing them en masse at only eighteen months old when their bodies can no longer stand the pressures of producing so many eggs.

Cheese comes from mother cows who have their newborn calves taken away from them year after year, until they too are slaughtered, is packaged and plastered with the image of a cartoonish, smiling cow. If you think about it, dairy production is very *The Handmaid's Tale*-esque.

Butchers sometimes even boast caricatures of pigs holding sausages, knives and the sliced-up flesh of their own species. Legs of pigs are sold wrapped in plastic in supermarkets that celebrate being 'sow-stall free', yet farrowing crates, another kind of small, metal-barred and concrete-floored enclosure, are standard in the pig industry. Mother pigs cannot turn around in them, and when their piglets are old enough, they're taken away from her to be grown and killed. The mother is inseminated again, and the whole process takes place yet again.

The language we use holds great power, as do the advertisements we assume to be truthful.

 **EXPLAINER**

Legal animal mutilations

Here are just some of the legal forms of mutilation that take place all across the world without any form of pain relief:

Animals harmed	Mutilation
Hens, chickens and turkeys	The tips of birds' beaks are seared off with extreme heat or infrared light
Turkeys	The ends of birds' toes are cut or seared off
Cattle, sheep and pigs	Animals' tails are cut off, most often with knives, sometimes scissors in the case of piglets
Calves, lambs and piglets	Animals' testicles are cut out, most often with knives, and sometimes tight bands that painfully cut off circulation
Piglets	The teeth of young piglets are cut out
Cattle	Horns and horn buds are either burned out with a hot iron cautery or cut with large cutting tools, causing bleeding

Castration takes place to control populations and to lower testosterone which can cause greater aggression. Animals confined in tight spaces together are more likely to act aggressively. Imagine you were crammed in a small space with other people, and you bumped into and treaded on each other due to tight confines – there's no doubt that this, combined with the frustration of deprivation in a windowless space, would result in fighting. These aggressions inevitably psychologically disturb animals – who sometimes also cannibalise or self-mutilate. And of course, if they don't have horns, clawed toes, tails to bite at, or teeth to bite with, then there's less bodily harm caused, and so more flesh and skin preserved for our eating and wearing.

# EXPLAINER

How we got here

Only 10,000 years ago, after 2.5 million years of gathering and occasionally hunting for our food, Yuval Noah Harari's research suggests that humans decided to do something else. It wasn't necessarily intentional, but we moved from eating a phenomenal array of different plants, to a select few staples. We also began to herd animals that we found easy to manipulate – gentle herbivores, those who wouldn't fight back too much and who could be bent to our will.

The ancient ancestors of today's sheep and goats were protected from non-human predators so that we could become their exclusive predators. We began to enclose the area where sheep and goats could be, while allowing only those species that were most submissive to live and breed. Any animal that was too aggressive in response to their new confinement or the killing of those around them wouldn't last.

Some of our human ancestors began to cut chunks out of pigs' snouts and tie thorns around calves' mouths so that it would hurt them to sniff and dig for food, and to suckle from their mother. We wanted to be the only hands that fed them, so we could control them. We wanted the milk for ourselves too. Today, metal rings are punctured through some free-range pigs' noses to prevent ground moving and digging, and chunks of their ears are cut out for identification. Plastic-thorned clips are still pushed into the noses of calves to prevent suckling.

Perhaps farming was never as picturesque as we imagine it to be, even so many years ago. Still, we like to imagine the humble, doting farmer who tends to his flock. We like to envision the red barn full of happy chickens who spend their days pecking for bugs in the grass, alongside wandering pigs who enjoy mud baths as a cow merrily moos over yonder.

This is a fantasy. Today, almost all chickens live in factory farms. In fact, according to the Sentience Institute, two thirds of animals on land do, and 90 per cent of all animals, when you include farmed fish, are confined to these spaces.

In 1923, Cecile Steele accidentally ordered 500 rather than fifty chickens she intended to sell eggs from. At the time, people didn't really exploit chickens for their flesh. Unable to fix her mistake, she shoved the birds into the sheds she had, and decided to sell them for slaughter. She realised this was making her more money than her original plan, and continued to order more chickens, until she had 10,000 ill-cared for chickens stuffed into her sheds. In the following fifty years, the previously non-existent chicken flesh industry killed three billion chickens every twelve months. Our obsession with eating animals continued to grow from then, and it has killed not only countless pigs, cows, sheep, chickens, ducks, turkeys, fish and other animals, but most anything close to the picturesque farms we like to imagine – that still, all profit from death.

How the law fails animals

At this point, a fair question to ask would be, 'How is any of this legal?' Well, across the United Kingdom, the United States, Australia, and most places in the world, farmed animals have no rights, and very few protections.

In Australia and the United States, farmed animals are specifically exempt from the wider protections other animals have – even if they are far and few between. Australia's Prevention of Cruelty to Animals Act lays out all the protections animals have, then specifically states that 'the Act does not apply' to 'any act or practice with respect to the farming, transport, sale or killing of any farm animal, which is carried out in accordance with a Code of Practice', which are mostly not mandatory and very weak. For example, blunt force killing of many animals is totally acceptable under these codes.

In America, we see that there are zero protections for animals on farms, but some protections for many animals – but not any bird species – in slaughterhouses. In Connecticut, a law that originally provided safety to 'all animals', now has been amended to make legal actions by anyone that 'maliciously and intentionally maim, mutilate, torture, wound or kill an animal, provided the act is done while following generally accepted agricultural practices'.

In the United Kingdom, farmed animals are only protected from 'unnecessary' harm and suffering. Suffering should be considered unnecessary if it is 'avoidable and if it is brought about purposefully'. That makes sense, right? But eating and wearing animals is avoidable, and the suffering we inflict upon animals we farm is absolutely purposeful. Basically, the commercialised harm and slaughter brought upon animals is considered by the law to be necessary. If you need to cut a piglet's teeth off so they don't bite each other while confined, it's fine.

Being farmed by humans means being entirely at our mercy – or serious lack of it.

 # ACTION

Use individualistic language

Consider the word 'it'. When you are talking about animals, or listening to other people speak about them, notice how often you hear the word 'it'.

'Look at that pig, it's limping', 'It's a chicken, it can't feel pain', 'It's just a fish', 'I wonder if the puppy misses its mother', 'It's fine, sheep are stupid'.

Even if the sentences are nice, 'Look at that cow, it looks so cute', the word 'it' is used to reference things, objects and commodities. Our language is powerful and it shifts our perception of the real world. When we refer to animals as objects, even if we are not consciously aware of it, we are upholding these ideas. We are perpetuating the notion that animals are in fact things, not individuals with feelings, thoughts and preferences.

It can be a challenge and it's okay to slip up, but try to refer to animals as 'he', 'she', or 'they' if you're not sure of the sex of the animal. You might find that the way you think of these animals might change too.

 # EXPLAINER

Free-range fraud

Free-range farming isn't common. In fact, for chickens slaughtered for their flesh – broilers – only one per cent of them are free-range farmed in America, according to the US National Chicken Council. That's less than one quarter of a per cent in Australia, according to Voiceless. Most chickens live in often windowless, crowded, ammonia-filled sheds that hurt your eyes if you walk into them. Most egg-laying hens around the world live in cages no bigger than an A4 sheet of printer paper. Rows upon rows of these cages are stacked high, full of noisy, stressed and even psychotic birds who are unable to cope with their confinement.

But let's say that free-range farming was common. What does it really look like? 'Free-range' is still undefined in many places, but in 2016, Australia introduced a legal definition for the term 'free-range' in relation to chickens which asks only for one square metre of space for each animal, and for 'meaningful and regular' outdoor access for animals, with these words not being defined.

One prominent chicken brand plays an ad with chickens roaming across rolling hills, a farmer tending to them with care. Yet chickens reared on farms owned by the brand, who are killed at about thirty-three days old, spend only fourteen of those days sometimes being provided access to the outdoors, according to the company. When they're not outside, they're crammed together, with up to twenty eight kilograms worth of chickens per square metre. Similar stories can be told of every other country around the world.

What if the animals really were free to graze on grass all day? A focus on 'free-range' in marketing helps us to forget all the other forms of exploitation animals on farms face. Sheep, for example, are generally free-range farmed animals, so it's often assumed that their lives are good ones. Yet in Australia, their tails can legally be cut off with a knife and no pain relief. We don't hear so much about that because it makes it harder to sell lamb flesh and wool.

We focus on how cows are fed grass rather than how cows have their horns painfully cut or burned off before they're killed. We remove the individuality from the cow. We call the cow 'it' and we call her flesh 'beef', her skin 'leather'. All of these words are more palatable, less genuine or reflective of what, or who, we are actually eating and wearing. Free-range is not only so often fraudulent, but a friendly face to look at while frighteningly cruel mutilations take place in these meadows.

ACTION

How language is used for the benefit of animal agriculture

Just like we call cow flesh 'beef' and cow skin 'leather', there are plenty of ways in which language is manipulated to make us more comfortable with animal exploitation, and to keep animal products in popularity. Here are just a few:

Profitable terminology	Reality
Bacon, pork, ham	Pig flesh
Beef	Cow flesh
Veal	Baby cow flesh
Mutton	Adult sheep flesh
Glycerine	Animal fat, normally from slaughtered cows and sheep (used in cosmetics and care products)
Slink leather	Leather from a newborn calf, or a calf nearly born, cut out of a heavily pregnant cow who is slaughtered
Lanolin	Grease excreted from the sebaceous glands of a sheep (used in cosmetics and care products)
K-leather	Kangaroo skin, often used in football boots
Gelatine	Boiled animal skin, tendons, cartilage and bones. Most often from pigs and cows.

Guanine	Pulverised fish scales (used in cosmetics to make them sparkle)
Milk	A term lobbyists in the EU are trying to ban the use of by companies selling any non-dairy milk like soy, oat and coconut milk
Burger	A term that lobbyists in the US and UK are trying to ban from being used by companies selling burgers made from anything plant-based
Sausage	Another word that is being discussed by governments, because apparently it's important that sausages sans meat instead be called 'protein tubes' or something
Leather	The German Leather Federation is having a crack at banning terms like 'vegan leather' or 'apple leather', even though 'leather' was once a made-up term too

Myth: Dairy isn't a slaughter industry, and cows need to be milked

Seemingly obvious but so often forgotten fact: cows must have been pregnant in order to produce milk, just like humans and every other mammal in the world. Milk exists for the purpose of raising newborns so they can grow quickly, to a point where they can eat solid foods. We stop needing milk when we stop drinking breast milk, and once we stop, milk production from breasts stop too. It's the same for calves and cows.

Most cows in the industrialised dairy industry are forcibly impregnated. Bulls, who are slaughtered once they are of no financial value, have a probe forced into their rectum, which stimulates them until they involuntarily ejaculate – the process is called 'electro-ejaculation', and the semen that comes from this is forced into a cow's uterus through artificial insemination, where a farmer forces their hand up their rectum and through into the vagina and cervix of the cow.

When calves are born, unless there has been genetic selection involved – which is rare – 50 per cent of them are male. They will of course, never produce milk, so they are slaughtered. Normally, this happens within five days of their birth, according to the RSPCA. They can legally be sent to slaughterhouses, shot with a rifle, or even hit with a hammer to the skull if they are less than twenty-four hours old.

Female calves stay with their mother briefly, and then are separated from them. Research published in WIRED shows that, unsurprisingly, calves become distressed and even depressed after this, and mother cows have been shown chasing the trucks and utes taking away their young. These calves are fed powdered milk, while mother cows and their udders are hooked to machines two or three times a day, for the sake of human consumption.

After some years of this, about seven, mother cows who have been pushed to their physical limits, no longer able to produce a profitable amount of milk, are slaughtered. It is not uncommon for cows to be slaughtered while pregnant, according to industry reports.

Myth: Eggs can be sourced ethically

Over generations, the hens we recognise today were selectively bred to have different traits than their ancestor, the red jungle fowl. This bird species lays between 10 to 15 eggs a year – not so different to my twelve annual periods, which makes sense, because an egg is released in both cases. Today, 'layer hens' ovulate almost every day of the year, releasing about 300 eggs according to the USDA. Clearly this is unnatural, and the impact of this cycle on hens is immense. Ex-egg industry hens who have been rescued often have surgery to remove shell-less eggs, membranes from old, unreleased eggs, and cysts in their oviduct. Hens begin laying a new egg when one is taken from them, and they are denied their time sitting on it. Many hens will eat their own eggs, especially when cracked open, helping them to regain some of the nutrients they lost.

All of this leads to the 'depopulation' of hens at eighteen months old. At this point, their bodies are exhausted, whether or not they've spent their lives in wire cages, in a large, windowless shed, or with some access to the outdoors. These chickens are sometimes sent to be slaughtered, but often, are killed in the way the industry claims is most 'humane' – gassing to death. Footage of this slow process shows birds panicking and gasping as they struggle to breathe, pass out, and die.

If being a female chicken sounds bad, being a male isn't so great either. The male chicks born in the industry – half, as with the dairy industry – are macerated soon after they are born. That means they are ground alive. In Australia, 12 million male chicks are ground alive every year. In the UK, it's 30 million, and in America, that number reaches the hundreds of millions. While some countries are developing technology that ensures males won't be born at all, the chickens and roosters who breed and birth these chicks, and the egg-laying hens themselves, all continue to be killed – whether or not the egg carton says 'free-range'.

When none of this is necessary, how can any of it be ethical?

 **ACTION**

Shop thoughtfully

* Buy certified free from animal testing, vegan cosmetics. Choose Cruelty Free has a great list covering these, and it's important to note that cosmetics certified as 'cruelty free' are not tested on animals, but might have animal ingredients in them (like animal fat, crushed bugs, wool grease from sheep sweat glands, and so on). Equally, products labelled 'vegan' may be tested on animals. There are plenty of brands – from those at the drugstore to fancy brands, that are both vegan and free from animal testing.

* Avoid leather, wool, cashmere, down, silk and other animal-derived materials as though they were fur. They all kill animals.

* Buy the more sustainable animal-material alternatives if you're able. While animal-derived materials are some of the most eco-impactful of all, some alternatives are better than others. For example, swap out your wool knit for an organic or recycled cotton, Tencel or hemp one, rather than a synthetic one. Helping the environment helps the free animals we share this planet with.

* Buy pre-loved. This is more affordable and sustainable than always buying new, making total ethics fashion accessible. Often we hear the argument that it's better to buy second-hand wool or leather goods rather than new vegan ones, but who's to stop you from buying second-hand or vintage vegan knitwear and leather?

* Mend and care for the clothes you have. These are the ones that you know won't do any more harm to animals, and they're the most sustainable.

# ACTION

See where your food and fashion purchases come from

If you'd rather see the issues within animal agriculture instead of reading about them, there are countless investigations and documentaries that reveal the reality of how we treat animals.

While these campaigns are from specific countries, the laws surrounding how animals are farmed and slaughtered are not so different across the world – and many of these incidents take place in countries with supposedly 'high animal welfare' laws:

Title	Subject
Dominion: The Documentary	Australian and global footage inside farms and slaughterhouses
Slay	Documentary about the use of animals in fashion
Earthlings	US footage inside farms and slaughterhouses, as well as animal testing facilities
Land of Hope and Glory	UK footage inside farms and slaughterhouses
Dairy is Scary – Animal Liberation	The treatment of calves in the dairy industry
Goat Truth – Animal Liberation Victoria	The treatment of kids in the dairy industry
Eggs Exposed – Farm Transparency Project	The treatment of male chicks in the industry. This organisation has a large number of excellent investigations.

Layer Hen Depopulation – Animal Liberation	The culling of all egg-laying hens at about 18 months old
This is the Truth About 'Humane' Free-Range Meat – Sentient	Footage from a free-range cattle farm in Australia
Videos That Will Change The Way You Think About Wool – PETA	Footage from over 116 wool-shearing operations and farms
There's Nothing Luxurious About Cashmere – PETA	Footage from cashmere farms and slaughter-houses. PETA also has investigations covering alpaca wool, down, exotic skins and more.
The Fur Trade – Humane Society International	Footage on fur farms
Drop Croc – Kindness Project	Footage on crocodile farms owned by luxury fashion houses
Willow & Claude, Subject	The issues with wool production and knitwear, and a path out of this

Of course, these videos are all graphic and disturbing so be warned. If it's not good enough for our eyes, should it be good enough for us to fund through our food and fashion purchases?

 # EXPLAINER

The wool industry

The wool industry is one which perhaps is most shrouded in myths of all that is ethical, wholesome and pure. It's also the industry I spend the most time thinking angrily about.

I have rescued a few newborn lambs, and spent many nights bottle feeding them milk, checking their temperatures and snuggling up with them. While it's very cute – though exhausting – I am not a sheep and so obviously not their actual mother. That's a problem: newborns are meant to be with their parents.

Yet, rescuers end up with so many lambs because in Australia, where the majority of wool, and particularly fine wool, comes from, 10–15 million newborn lambs die in the first forty-eight hours of their life every winter lambing season. They die of starvation, neglect and exposure to the cold.

They die because lambs, like many animals, should be born into spring. They are bred into winter as it means reduced feed costs for farmers, who fatten up lambs for slaughter on spring grass months later. They also die because their mothers have been selectively bred to birth twins and even triplets, when that is as naturally common for sheep as it is for humans. When mother ewes are not able to physically cope with these pregnancies, they can prolapse and die. Sometimes, they choose which lamb they think is strongest and have to abandon the weaker of the two or three, in hopes of caring for one of them successfully.

The lambs who survive have their tails cut off, and their testicles if they are male. Sometimes, they are still legally mulesed – the skin on their rear sliced off with a knife. This practice is controversial and discussions about banning it have happened for decades – though some industry members are concerned that demanding pain relief for mulesing, will mean people will demand pain relief for tail docking and other practices too. (Good heavens, how terrible!)

Some sheep are slaughtered as young lambs, shorn before their death. Others are killed without being shorn, so their woolly skins can be sold and made into boots, slippers and jackets. The sheep with the highest quality wool are often kept for 'wool-growing', and are shorn at least once a year – sometimes in the cold of winter – so we can keep warm with their wool. Shearing is often extremely violent, and over 116 wool operations have been documented and exposed for extreme cruelty.

After five or six years, about half the natural lifespan of a sheep, wool production slows and these sheep are slaughtered too. Yes, the wool industry is a slaughter industry, with even Merino sheep being described as 'dual-purpose', used for their flesh and wool.

There are plenty of better materials to stay cosy with that would be approved by rescued lambs. These are the individuals we need to think of when we go to buy any sweater or scarf.

 # ACTION

Hold yourself to your values

There's a whole lot of information to absorb in this chapter, and learning about just how terribly we treat other species on this planet can be phenomenally confronting, even traumatising. So many of us consider ourselves animal lovers, and knowing that such everyday things like our meals and our outfits can do such harm to such sensitive creatures is overwhelming.

The thing to do with all of this knowledge, and with all of the feelings we have about it, is decide what we want to do with it all. What are our values? Do these materials and foods, and this industry align with them?

Your thoughts may be different from someone else's, but it's important to choose our own personal code of ethics, over what is sometimes just a little bit more convenient.

Write down a list of the things you might like to do differently, think of ways you can align your actions with your sense of what is right.

✳ Choosing to look directly at the injustices around us is uncomfortable, and evolving into a more ETHICAL way of living can be challenging. The most UNCOMFORTABLE thing we can do to ourselves though, is sit in the knowledge that our actions are not aligning with our own sense of what is RIGHT, JUST and FAIR

Chapter Six

ANIMAL ISSUES ARE OUR ISSUES

Humans are animals

When thinking about how veganism can save us, it's worth considering that because speciesism is a type of discrimination built upon the idea of human superiority over animals, it can build upon the fallacy that we are not animals ourselves. It can be easy for us to forget because we live so differently to other animal species, but we are. We are human animals. Humans who live in apartments, fish who spend their entire lives in the deep sea, birds who spend much of their time flying and moles who like to be underground, all live differently, and are all equally animal. Yet, because the way we live has been decided to be more 'evolved', we see ourselves as only partially animal today, mostly something else, something greater.

So let's look at evolution. Let's go back 530 million years ago to when fish with backbones started hanging out here on Earth. That was a cool moment. Thirty million years later, the first animals came onto land, and they looked something like a crustacean mixed with the insects of today. Some 440 million years ago, some of the bony fish split and evolved into new types of fish, until 397 million years ago, the first four-legged animal came up onto land, and made way for all amphibians, birds, reptiles and mammals. This animal is probably descended from the tiktaalik. Over many millions of years, primates came about and evolved into all the different species we know today – orangutans, gibbons, gorillas and so on. A comparatively short time ago in the scheme of things, around 6 million years ago some chimpanzees and bonobos changed things up so much that they evolved into those we consider prehistoric 'humans' today.

We consider this the 'apex' of evolution. Humans came to be and the animals who are our closest relatives are admired because they're close to our supposed human glory. But when did we decide 'latest to evolve' meant 'greatest'? Why? Far more recently, fierce wolves evolved – through manipulation – into small dogs with faces so short they struggle to breathe properly. Eagles have been around for longer than pigeons, as have great white sharks compared to salmon fish. Crocodiles have been around far longer than the kittens we think are cute. Are these enormous, strong species less evolved? Yes, they have changed less over time, been around for longer than the other species. Is 'less evolved' interchangeable with 'worse'? 'Less' interesting, important, worthy, sentient, animal? No. We're all just different animals, with different arrival times, different lineages, different features, abilities and ways of life.

If we are ever to see some kind of genuine peace on this planet, we must remember that we are animals, in a shared environment. We have an obligation to look after it, and each other.

To think a world without exploitation of non-human animals can exist where racism, sexism, ableism and LGBTQ+ discrimination still exists is ignoring the root of why animals are exploited

lauren T Ornelas

Oppression built upon the identity of human

I spoke to Christopher Sebastian, a Black writer and liberation activist on how the oppression of humans and other animals is connected. He says that 'everyone probably understands "human" as a biological classification, but it was actually white supremacy that set up "human" as a political identity'. White supremacy deems some humans more worthy of rights than others based on their skin colour, but more, based on a perceived 'animality', or lack of 'humanity'. Historically, and shockingly sometimes still today, Sebastian notes that Black people are considered some kind of missing link between the non-human species humans evolved from – only sort-of humans. Oppression is often rooted in dehumanising individuals, and this is because we fear being animalised. In some ways, we fear being closer to nature.

Being animal is considered being bad – we often refer to those humans who commit horrific and vicious crimes as 'animals'. This is because our constructed hierarchy among humans is like a leaderboard in who is 'most human'. Those considered 'sub-human', because of their race, their disability or even their gender expression are condemned to be treated as inferior. In this hierarchy, the 'most human' are the 'most evolved', and these are, supposedly, white human males, in our white supremacist, speciesist, patriarchal world.

The political identity of 'human' then exists to elevate cis-gendered white men above everyone else, to push people out of imaginary boxes of supposed worth. Whether someone is human, Black, Brown, feminine, queer, trans, disabled, or anything else, they are not 'normal', not a standard 'human', and so less than human. They are closer to being an animal.

Headlines referring to human rights issues seen in detention centres and prisons often refer to animals, stating that these humans are 'treated like animals', and that that is disgusting and unethical. The idea here, is to show that of course these humans deserve better treatment than animals, simply because they are humans. The intention of such headlines is good – all humans deserve fairness and justice. However, it perpetuates the idea that such treatment is acceptable for animals, and that humans are separate from every other species on the planet – better, deserving more safety and freedom.

Grappling with the reality that we are animals is confronting, because of this. Particularly for Black, Indigenous and people of colour who continue to be referred to as animals for the purpose of justifying violence towards them. However, our concern with proving our humanity, of 'humanising' ourselves, 'leads at once to the recognition of dehumanisation', and the risks that come with this. Dehumanisation simply would not be a tool for oppression if we were comfortable in our animality, as Sebastian says we ought to be. And of course, we can never be comfortable in our human animal identity, if violence is justified towards anyone labelled 'animal'. Until speciesism is dismantled, nor will dehumanisation and resulting injustice.

We need another and a wiser and perhaps a more mystical concept of animals. Remote from universal nature, and living by complicated artifice, man in civilisation surveys the creature through the glass of his knowledge and sees thereby a feather magnified and the whole image in distortion. We patronise them for their incompleteness, for their tragic fate of having taken form so far below ourselves. And therein we err, and greatly err. For the animal shall not be measured by man ... They are not brethren, they are not underlings; they are other nations, caught with ourselves in the net of life and time, fellow prisoners of the splendour and travail of the earth

Henry Beston

ACTION

Further reading on intertwined oppression and collective liberation

There are many voices speaking about the importance of work towards collective liberation for all. When oppression is such a twisted, thorny and complex problem to solve, we need voices and ideas from all different kinds of people to help break it down.

If you're looking for anti-speciesist perspectives on this kind of thing, there are some great people, books and resources below:

✳ Christopher Sebastian
(excellent articles and talks available through his website)

✳ Iye Bako (great resources through her social media, @iyeloveslife)

✳ *Beasts of Burden: Animal and Disability Liberation*
by Sunaura Taylor

✳ *The Dreaded Comparison: Human and Animal Slavery*
by Marjorie Spiegel

✳ Yvette Baker (@vegan_abolitioniste on Instagram,
shares important resources and thoughts)

✳ *Five Essays For Freedom* by Kristy Alger

✳ The Afro Vegan Society

✳ The written works of Aph and Syl Ko

✳ The written works of A. Breeze Harper PhD, particularly *Sister Species*, *Sistah Vegan* and her chapter in *Cultivating Food Justice*

✳ The Beyond Species podcast

We cannot be
against violence
sometimes, or against
injustice sometimes.
Oppression is a
structure, and we must
work to recognise
it in all of its forms,
so we can ACT
and DISMANTLE it
accordingly

 # EXPLAINER

Consistent anti-oppression and environmental justice

So what does it mean to be consistent with our values? Assuming we are indeed opposed to oppression (if not ... what's up?), being consistent with our values means recognising and interrogating oppression wherever we see it, not only when we see specific symptoms of this unjustly hierarchical system. It means looking beyond a singular 'ism' – environmentalism, racism, sexism, speciesism, and recognising the way oppression casts a shadow across us all, and the very Earth we share.

When we recognise oppression rather than only symptoms of it, we are better equipped to dismantle it. We are better able to understand the roots, and hack away at them.

When we are consistently against oppression, the way we advocate for a better world also changes. It would no longer make sense to sell t-shirts supporting an LGBTQ+ charity if they were made under modern slavery conditions, from materials hurting the planet. It would no longer make sense to hold a barbeque of cooked animal flesh to raise funds for wild animals impacted by bushfires, or for locked up refugees – when these sausages are contributing to the warming of our planet, and made from confined individuals, too.

Everyone is constantly learning, and consistent anti-oppression is not about perfectionism. However, it is about a willingness to broaden our understanding of how discrimination operates, as well as extending our circle of compassion to those we did not deem worthy previously.

The term 'environmental justice' is a good one to consider here, as this is a justice that recognises we are all a part of nature, and all deserve protection. Environmental justice seeks not only to protect the environment, in terms of trees, forests, waterways and grasslands, but those who live in it. Do the non-human and human beings living in and around these spaces have access to what they need for a healthy, happy life? Is there enough natural environment around us for a good life? The wellbeing of the environment is our wellbeing, and our responsibility.

# ACTION

Put collective liberation into action

How can we ensure that our work for some does not mean harm for others? How can we tie together environmental, non-human and human protection? How can we articulate that the liberation we are working for is not exclusive, not built upon the disenfranchisement of someone else? When we keep the idea of collective liberation core to our work, this becomes easier.

Some examples of ways to create more collectively liberating actions include:

* Helping to create and support food justice which considers access for marginalised communities, animal-free foods that protect non-humans, decent and fair farm-worker rights, and environmentally friendly options. This could be through choosing fair-trade foods like chocolate, choosing vegan foods and cooking them for those in need, supporting community gardens, fridges and pantries.
* Protesting, writing letters to members of government, and to organisations that are supporting and paying for environmental destruction. This could be land clearing for grazing, a polluting factory farm, a mine or other proposed destruction that would impact Indigenous communities, wild animals and the health of the planet we all share.
* Ensuring that the language we use when we speak about any social justice issue is not harmful to another community.

* Sharing information with your community about social and environmental justice issues they might not have considered before, especially when such issues intertwine with those they're already concerned by.
* Considering what voices are not being heard, and how they can be amplified. Collective liberation is not about being a hero, but about mutual support. Make the spaces you move in welcoming to everyone.
* There's nothing wrong with having a main area of focus or passion when it comes to collective liberation, but it is important we keep in mind other causes, how they all intersect and how we need to support each other, not 'compete for liberation'.

I usually don't mention I'm **VEGAN** but that has evolved … I think it's the right moment to talk about it, because it is part of a **REVOLUTIONARY PERSPECTIVE**

Angela Davis

We can save ourselves, together

When we ask how veganism can save us, we're asking how we can save us.

We're talking about the individual choices and actions we can make when it comes to sitting down for a meal, getting dressed and engaging with our community, our environment. There's no single way to save the planet, or to solve the many issues we face today. But the benefit of veganism is that changes that – in the scheme of things – are not so huge, have an enormous, wide-reaching impact.

The next time you're looking at boots online, if you choose to not buy leather, you could be contributing your small part in the protection of the Amazon Rainforest, thereby also standing in support of the work of Indigenous Amazon protectors. If you go for vegan bolognese instead of a beef burger or chicken schnitzel, you save greenhouse gas emissions and pollution from changing our atmosphere. All of these choices are, of course, far better for animals too.

Veganism isn't just a diet or a lifestyle; it's a way to help create the change you want to see in the world. It's a way to ease the burden and pain of individuals and the planet.

If you choose to start eating, dressing and living vegan, that alone won't save us. No single action or person can. Fortunately, it's not just you and I here on the planet. There are billions of us who are able to work together to make a difference, whether that be through conversation, direct action or personal changes.

We each need to decide what we are willing to change, for all our sakes. And we need to start now.

References

For all references please head to Emma's website via this QR code.

Thank you

Firstly, I'm thankful for you, person reading this book. Thank you for your openness in extending your circle of compassion, and for taking whatever actions you do next.

Next, I'm very grateful to have had the opportunity to write this book. Thank you to Hardie Grant, and to Alice Hardie Grant in particular, for believing in the importance of bringing a more radical (but when you think about it, really not that radical) 'version' of veganism into the mainstream.

Thank you to Libby Turner for being a kind and diligent editor, and thank you to my Mum, for being the unofficial and lovingly brutal editor of so many things I write, before I let anyone else see them.

This book wouldn't be what it is without the input from so many people quoted and referenced in this book – please do head to the QR code and dive into the many references included in here, there is so much amazing work to explore. In particular, I want to thank Christopher Sebastian who, in the space of maybe an hour on Zoom, spoke so eloquently yet casually about such important issues that he, without perhaps realising, helped me to profoundly shift how I think about the world.

I'm grateful to every animal advocate, every collective liberation activist in my life, for giving me hope for a better world.

Last of all, I am so thankful to every non-human animal who has truly honoured me with the chance to get to know them, even when their lives up until our meeting have been filled with such incredible betrayal, injustice and hurt. I've learnt so much about how to be a better human from my fellow animals.

Published in 2022 by Hardie Grant Books, an imprint of Hardie Grant Publishing

Hardie Grant Books (Melbourne)
Wurundjeri Country
Building 1, 658 Church Street
Richmond, Victoria 3121

Hardie Grant Books (London)
5th & 6th Floors
52–54 Southwark Street
London SE1 1UN

hardiegrantbooks.com

 A catalogue record for this book is available from the National Library of Australia

NATIONAL LIBRARY OF AUSTRALIA

How Veganism Can Save Us
ISBN 9781743797730

10 9 8 7 6 5 4 3 2 1

Commissioning Editor: Alice Hardie-Grant
Editor: Libby Turner
Design Manager: Kristin Thomas
Designer: Ngaio Parr Studio
Production Manager: Todd Rechner
Production Coordinator: Jessica Harvie

Colour reproduction by Splitting Image Colour Studio
Printed in China by Leo Paper Products LTD.

Hardie Grant acknowledges the Traditional Owners of the country on which we work, the Wurundjeri people of the Kulin nation and the Gadigal people of the Eora nation, and recognises their continuing connection to the land, waters and culture. We pay our respects to their Elders past and present.

Survive the Modern World

Upskill and expand your knowledge with these accessible pocket guides.

Available now

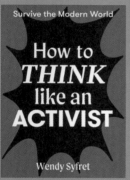

Survive the Modern World

How to **THINK** like an **ACTIVIST**

Wendy Syfret

Survive the Modern World

How *to start* A SIDE Hustle

Kaylene Langford

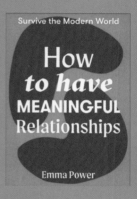

Survive the Modern World

How *to have* MEANINGFUL Relationships

Emma Power

Survive the Modern World

How *to be* ONLINE & also be HAPPY

Issy Beech

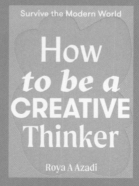

Survive the Modern World

How *to be a* CREATIVE Thinker

Roya A Azadi